Crossroads Country Recipes

Copyright © by Itterman Sisters
First Edition - November 1998
Second Printing - February 1999

Cover Design by: Klatt Laser Graphics
                            Sherwood Park, AB Canada

Typeset and Design by: Karen Shepherd
                            Edmonton, AB Canada

Photography by: Mike Copeman Photography
                            Fort Saskatchewan, AB Canada

Printed by: Jasper Printers
                            Edmonton, AB Canada

Published and Distributed by: Itterman Sisters

Dedication

Dedicated to the memory of "Mom" Olga Itterman - nee Zeitner - 1903 - 1992.

Who taught us by example, Christian values and how to use our gifts of hospitality.

We remember your love, demonstrated by welcoming all into our home, to the aroma of freshly brewed coffee and homemade bread and kuchen.

We pay tribute and say "thanks" to Mom and Dad for the rich heritage, for truly this is what has kept us seven children together.

Come Gather at our Table

When entering Mom's kitchen - you were handed an apron. The apron had many uses besides protecting the dress. Mom would use hers to wipe our tears when we were hurt, use the edge of the apron to dust a table as visitors arrived. She used it for a grip enhancer for opening mason jars, carry in vegetables, wood from the shed and eggs from the hen house.

Today the line of duty for aprons has changed, from protection to collection.

Her aprons symbolized hard work, comforting words and good food.

Introduction

Crossroads, that little school house that stood many years on the Saskatchewan prairies brings back many memories. Maybe it was those jam sandwiches we carried to school for lunch in honey and syrup pails, that has given us a quest for compiling this book. How things have changed.

We've chosen the name "CROSSROADS" because that was the school for all of us in our early years. We truly have fond recollections of that little country schoolhouse. Life has taken us in many directions and yet our paths have crossed often in joyous and sad occasions. Important to us is the symbol of the cross, significant of life.

This book is one way of passing on our heritage to our children and grandchildren. These recipes have become our favourites, some originally received from family and friends - we say thanks. This has definitely turned out to be a larger task than anticipated. The support and input of our husbands - Elmer - Gordon - Don and Roy has been greatly appreciated, many times they were used as critiques.

Those recipes from Mom that had a pinch of this, a dab of that, butter the size of an egg or your little finger, just wasn't accurate enough. Thro laughter and tears, we did it, so here it is - the book

"Crossroads Country Recipes"

comprised by four sisters.

Elma - **Ebea**

Ann - **Enae**

Alice - **Elyce**

Sylvia - **Elly**

5

Life is like a Tapestry

Life is like a tapestry, the design is our own choosing,
Depending on the fabric - and the type of thread we're using.

Each day we weave a portion, and at first it's hard to see,
Just what the final picture - of our weaving is to be.

We oft begin with confidence, a picture in our mind,
But if we are not careful - our stitches will unwind.

Let strong "FAITH" frame your canvas, God wants this work to last,
And it's hard to change the color - once the final dye is cast.

Each day will bring new colors, red for "JOY" and peaceful white,
Others may bring different hues - to contrast with the light.

Some days the colors will be dark, and tinged with blue and grey,
Then you'll need a hope strong thread - to see you thro the day.

And when we make an error, don't walk away and leave it,
The picture will be stronger - in the spot where you reweave it.

Life's loom is never idle, you have the shuttle in your hand,
With threads of love and laughter - the final picture will be grand.

God grant us strength and courage, life's canvas seems so vast,
And the little bit we stitch to-day- could be our very last.

My picture is almost finished, I'll soon put my tools away,
May the tapestry I leave behind - help another on life's way.

By Leona Chugg
Used by Permission

6

Contents

Celebrations Year Round   8

Alpha & Omega   18

The Weekender   38

The Bakery   56

Crowning Glories   118

That Extra Touch   140

Versatile Dishes   152

The Salad Bar   174

The Meat Market   196

Celebrations Year Round

Menus
Basics
How-To

Christmas - New Year

Roast Turkey: Dressing - Cranberries - Mashed Potatoes - Gravy - Yummy Yams - Vegetable and Relish Plate (Carrot Sticks - Celery) Jewel Cranberry Salad - Broccoli Salad Delight - Kernel Corn - Christmas Pudding with Caramel Sauce - Chocolate Cream Roll - Pies - Apple - Pecan - Mincement or Pumpkin

Easter Dinner

Glazed Baked Ham - Pineapple Rings
Scalloped Potatoes - Glazed Carrots - Yum Yum Salad
Frozen Pineapple Nut Salad - Lemon Pie
Fruit Cocktail Dessert with Whipped Cream

Mothers Day

Barbecued Chicken (Marinated) - Hash Brown Bake
Peas and Carrots - Fresh Fruit Salad - Strawberry Shortcake
Dinner Roll - Punch

Fathers Day

Barbecued Steaks (Marinated) - Baked Potatoes with Sour Cream
Corn - Plum Creek Salad - Dinner Roll - Punch
Cheesecake or Apple Pie a-la-mode.

Thanksgiving

Roast Turkey - Dressing - Cranberries - Mashed Potatoes - Gravy
Itterman Cabbage Rolls - Pyrogies with Sour Cream
Yummy Yams - Nut Pudding Salad - Layered 24 Hour Lettuce Salad
Cauliflower - Green Peas or Beans - Pumpkin or Pecan Pie -
Decadent Apricot Cheesecake

Menus

Baked Fish or Pan Fried:
Boiled Potatoes - Ma's Coleslaw - Sliced Tomatoes - Tartar Sauce -
Green Beans - Rice Pudding

Barbecued Hamburgers:
Potato Salad - Bean Salad - Strawberry Cream Salad - Veggie Tray
with Dip - Chocolate Cream Pie or Springtime Cake

Barbecued Steaks:
Baked Potatoes - Baked Onions - Fried Mushrooms - Caesar Salad -
Raisin Pie - Peanut Buster Parfait

Beef Stew with Dumplings:
Fresh Crusty Bread - Garden Salad - Flapper Pie

Canton Noodle Dish:
French Bread - Marinated Vegetable Salad - Raisin Cake with
Caramel Sauce

Chicken Cordon Bleu:
Whipped Potato Bake - Pickled Crabapples - Broccoli Dish - Dinner
Rolls - Cherry Cheesecake Supreme

Chili:
Carrot Sticks - Corn Bread - Fruit Cocktail Dessert

Elly's Glorious Chicken:
Mashed Potatoes - Green Beans - Plain Fruit Salad - Banana Split
Dessert

Elyce's Sunday Chicken:
Broccoli Salad Delight - Corn - Dinner Rolls - Lemon Jello Dessert

Farmers Sausage:
Pyrogies - Kleice or Buttered Noodles - Green Bean Mandarin -
Applesauce - Peach Halves - Saucy Raisin Pudding

Ginger Chicken:
Steamed Rice - Carrots - 24 Hour 5 Cup Salad - Rhubarb Meringue
Dessert or Butter Tarts with Ice Cream

Glazed Rack of Ribs:
Stuffed Baked Potatoes - Frozen Mixed Vegetables - Caesar Salad - French Vanilla Torte

Kotletten - Hamburgers:
Peas and Carrots - Creamy Lettuce - Mashed Potatoes - Chocolate Fudge Pudding.

Lasagna:
Tossed Salad - French Bread - Saucy Raisin Pudding

Meat Loaf:
Baked Potatoes - Corn or Green Beans - Tossed Garden Salad - Garlic Toast - Layered Mousse Dessert or Sherbet

Mexican Casserole:
Green Salad - Corn on the Cob - Dinner Rolls - Black Forest Cake

Oma's Beef Roast:
Mashed Potatoes - Gravy - Glazed Carrots - Dinner Rolls - Plum Creek Salad - Lovelight Cake served with Strawberries and Ice Cream

Oma's Sauerkraut with Barley:
Mashed Potatoes - Bread Pudding with Sauce

Pepper Steak:
Steamed Rice - Pea Salad - Baking Powder Biscuits - Strawberry Pie or Brownies with Ice Cream and Chocolate Sauce

Pork Chops:
Plain or with Mushroom Gravy - Applesauce - Sliced Potato Bake - Sweet -Sour Cabbage - Dinner Rolls - Chocolate Pie

Porkies:
Scalloped Potatoes - Peas or Beans - Pistachio Salad or Tossed Salad - Fruit Cocktail Dessert

Prime Rib Roast:
Yorkshire Pudding - Mashed Potatoes - Gravy - Buttered Peas and Carrots - Creamy Fruit Salad - Horseradish - Decadent Apricot Cheesecake

Roast Pork:
Mashed Potatoes - Gravy - Broccoli Bake - Cinnamon Applesauce or Whipped Cream Apple Salad - Poppyseed Cake

Salmon Loaf:
Hashbrown Bake - Coleslaw - Harvard Beets - Lemon Jello Dessert

Seasoned Baked Chicken:
Baked Potatoes with Sour Cream - Corn on the Cob - Holiday Salad - Chocolate Cream Pie or Springtime Cake

Sloppy Joe's:
Buns - Potato Chips - Italian Garden Salad - One Bowl Chocolate Cake or Fresh Fruit

Stroganoff:
Egg Noodles - Steamed Broccoli - Oriental Cabbage Salad - Triffle

Sweet and Sour Ribs:
Steamed Rice - Peas - Yum Yum Salad - Apple pie

Wai-ki-ki Meat Balls:
Steamed Rice - Kernel Corn - Garden Salad - Strawberry Shortcake

Basics - How To

Bacon - Time Saver
Brown a pound of bacon - cool - crumble and freeze in small amounts - use as needed.

Beef Stock:

3 lbs.	beef bones	2 1/2 tsp.	salt
2	onions quartered	5	peppercorns
2	carrots quartered		Bouquet Garni =
3 pcs.	celery stocks		(parsley-thyme-bay leaf)

NOTE: Bouquet Garni - herbs placed together in a cheesecloth and tied with a string.
Place into a large pot with enough water to cover - bring to a slow boil - simmer 1 - 2 hours till meat falls off bones. Skim occasionally -strain the stock - use as desired.

Butter:
Contributes flavor - freshness - tenderness. Flavored butter may be used to pour over or dress up vegetables - meats - bread or popcorn.
Ex. garlic - parsley - cheese - tarragon - basil - thyme - curry.

Clarified Butter:
Butter heated without burning. Set aside - carefully skim off the white foamy butter fat that rises to the top - clear liquid is the clarified butter. May be stored in the fridge and used on vegetables.

Chicken Stock:
Use giblets - neck - heart - gizzard - wing tips and backs etc. NEVER ADD LIVER = IT GIVES A BAD TASTE - use the same ingredients and method as for preparing beef stock except for the meat replacement.

Chocolate Curls:
Solid chocolate should be at room temperature - shave off thin slices using a sharp knife or vegetable peeler.

How to Melt Chocolate:
Melt in a heavy saucepan over low heat - stirring often - MICROWAVE - 1 ounce of chocolate - may take 1 - 2 mins. - till soft enough to stir smooth.

Corn Starch: 1 tablespoon   =   2 tbsp. flour
Corn Starch needs to be mixed with a little cold water before adding to thicken sauces - gravies and puddings.

Creme Fraiche:
Topping for chocolate desserts (more tart than whipping cream). Measure equal amounts of whipping cream and sour cream. Stir together - cover - let stand in a warm place 12 hours. Stir and refrigerate 24 hours. - Special and delicious.

Eggs - Boiled
Place in a saucepan - cover with water - bring to a boil. Turn off heat - cover with a lid - let sit on the element for 10 minutes.

Eggs Separated:
Whites will keep in the refrigerator for about a week or may be frozen.

Whites - mean lower cholesterol:
Whites are used for meringues. Whites are beaten with a mixer till they form stiff peaks and sugar has been added. Yolks may be stored in a jar - covered with water - and a lid. Will keep up to 3 days in the refridgerator. To remove - lift gently with a slotted spoon. A small amount of yolk in egg whites will prevent whites from beating properly.

Flour:
Should be stored in a dry place. For an accurate - measurement - dip 1 cup measure into flour till over flowing - use back of a knife blade to scrape straight across to level cup. DO NOT PACK OR SHAKE.

Flour and Eggs:
Build a foundation when used in a cake.

Fruit:
To prevent browning when peeling - dip in lemon or pineapple juice or drop into salted cold water. **Skins** from peaches or tomatoes can be removed if you pour boiling water over fruits - allow to stand 30 seconds - skins will come off easily.

Fruit Stains:
Stains on hands or fish odors can be removed if rubbed with lemon juice.

Lemons and Oranges:
Will squeeze easier - if you roll on counter top to soften or microwave for one minute.

Garlic: 1 large clove =   1 tsp. minced garlic
To peel and store - cut off ends - lay flat side of a knife on garlic clove - press down hard to crush. Skins will come off easily - mince fine - TO STORE - place in a jar - cover with salad oil. Cover with a tight fitting lid store in refrigerator. Oil in the jar can be used for flavor in salads.

Gelatine:
One envelope of Knox Gelatine sets: 2 cups of liquid or 1 1/2 cups of solids.

Gravy: Beef - Chicken - Pork
The base of a good gravy is the sediment left in the roasting pan to which water or stock is added. Tilt the roasting pan - skim off excess fat with a spoon. Add 1 1/2 - 2 cups of stock or water - bring to a boil - scraping the sediment off bottom of pan. For the thickening agent place into a jar or shaker: 1 cup cold water - add 4 tsp. flour - cover and shake till smooth. Bring stock in pan to a boil - slowly stir in flour mixture - cook till thick. Add a little extra water if needed - season with salt and pepper. If extra flavor is needed - add dry soup base granules. You can purchase gravy browning color in a bottle to give the gravy a desired color.

Ham Broth:
Use one ham bone with some meat left on - 1 bay leaf and 1/2 onion quartered. Place into a saucepan - cover with water - bring to a boil - reduce heat - simmer one hour. Strain the broth - take meat off bone. Cover and store in refrigerator till needed or make soup.

Muffins:
Use an ice cream scoop to fill paper cups or pans.

Pies:
Slits in the top of a pie are steam vents. To dress up a double crust pie - brush the top crust with a mixture of a lightly beaten egg and 1 tbsp. milk - sprinkle sugar over top. To thaw and re-heat a frozen pie - place it into a cold oven. Set oven heat to 350° for 30 minutes. A flakier pie crust can be obtained if using lemon soda or orange juice instead of the usual liquids in the recipe.

Potatoes - To Boil and Mash
Peel potatoes - cut to desired size - place into a saucepan. Add enough water to cover and 1 tsp. salt per six servings. Boil till fork tender - drain off water. Mash with a potato masher or beater until there are no more lumps. Add enough milk so potatoes are fluffy and not dry. Top with butter or grated cheese - opt.
Note: Potato water may be used for liquids in gravy.

Sauces:
To prevent lumps when using flour or corn starch you need to stir constantly. Cook over low to medium heat unless recipe states otherwise. Cook only as long as specified - OVER COOKING can cause sauces to curdle or break down. If you need to leave the sauce while cooking - remove from heat.

Sour Milk: 1 cup portion - Into a measuring cup put 1 tbsp. vinegar or lemon juice. Fill cup with milk to full measure - let stand 5 minutes before using. (Buttermilk may be used in place of sour milk.)

Sugar: Granulated sugar should be spooned into measuring cup. Brown sugar should be pressed firmly into measuring cup. Sugar used in baking adds color - MOISTURE and volume. **Caramelized sugar** - place granulated sugar into a heavy skillet or saucepan. Place over medium heat without stirring till it begins to melt - shake saucepan occasionally. Reduce heat to low - cook stirring frequently till golden brown and completely melted. May be used to give nuts a candy coating.
NOTE: Powdered, Icing or Confectioners Sugar are the same.

Vegetables: To blanch before freezing - place into boiling water - allow to sit 3 mins. - remove to an ice water bath to cool quickly.

Vinegar:
Adds zip without adding salt. Vinegar is used in preparing foods in different ways. Salad dressings - marinades and many household uses.

Whipping Cream: _How To_ - 1 cup whipping cream chilled plus 4 tbsp. icing sugar and 1 tsp. vanilla. Place ingredients into a chilled bowl - beat till stiff. Whipped cream should be double in volume - fluffy and smooth. If you add 1 tsp. of instant vanilla pudding to one cup of whipping cream when whipping in advance of using - it will keep much longer in the refrigerator and not turn thin and milky in the bottom. May be frozen in mounds for use.

Yeast:
Two different kinds called for in recipes. _Traditional Dry Yeast:_ Soak in warm water 40°C or 105°F plus sugar. Amount of yeast - sugar and water as recipe specifies. Yeast should foam lightly before adding to other ingredients. Allow approx. 10 minutes. _Instant Yeast:_ Mix with flour - add directly to batter - making sure liquids are not to hot - so as not to kill the action of the yeast. Beating well is important.

To Season a New Fry Pan: Wash it well - dry and cover the bottom with oil and salt. Let stand 12 hours - then heat the oil till very hot. Take off heat - pour out oil - wipe pan thoroughly with paper towels while still hot. Usually this pan should not have to be washed after using but wiped with a damp cloth dipped in salt. This should be done while pan is still warm.

Notes:

Alpha & Omega

Appetizers
Beverages
Candy

Cheese Dip

1 lb.	ground beef
1 lb.	Velveeta cheese - melted
1 tin	enchilada sauce - medium size
1 sm. can	hot peppers chopped - amount opt.

Brown meat; drain well - add the rest of the ingredients.

Serve over fondue heat.

Use as a dip. Can use chunks of bread, nachos or raw veggies

Cheese Ball

1-8 oz.	cream cheese - room temperature
8 oz.	old cheddar cheese - shredded
2 tbsp.	minced onion
2 tsp.	lemon juice
1 tbsp.	worcestershire sauce
1/2 tsp.	crushed garlic - optional
	cracked pepper - optional
	walnuts - chopped
	parsley

Mix together in food processor or mixer - cream cheese - cheddar cheese - onion - lemon juice - garlic and sauce.
Shape into a ball.

Roll ball in either walnuts - parsley or cracked pepper.
Serve with an assortment of crackers or melba toast.

Why is a cook book exciting?

Because it has many stirring events.

Hot Artichoke Dip

1 lge. can	unmarinated artichoke hearts - chopped
1 sm. can	sliced black olives
1 sm. can	diced green chiles
1 1/2 cup	mayonnaise
1 1/2 cup	parmesan cheese
	dash of pepper

Mix together - put into a baking dish.
Bake @ 425° for 20 mins.

Serve with tortilla chips.

Elyce's Hot Chicken Wings

2 lbs.	chicken wings	1 tbsp.	honey
1/4-1/3cup	hot sauce	1 tsp.	lemon juice
1 tbsp.	tabasco sauce	2 tbsp.	barbecue sauce

Deep fry wings, drain on paper towel - set aside.

Combine other ingredients in a saucepan - boil 5 mins.

Remove from heat - toss wings in sauce to coat.

Veggie Dip

1 cup	sour cream	1 tsp.	bon appetite
1/2 cup	Miracle Whip	1 tsp.	dill weed
1 tsp.	onion powder	1 tsp.	parsley

In a bowl combine all ingredients - stir well to mix.

Cover and refrigerate for several hours or overnight before serving with a tray of your favourite vegetables.

Salmon Pate

1 can	salmon	1-8 oz. pkg.	cream cheese
1/4 cup	grated onion	1 1/2 tbsp.	lemon juice
1/2 tsp.	liquid smoke	1 tsp.	dill weed

Mix together until blended, shape into a ball, serve with crackers.

Fruit Dip

| 1/2 cup | whipping cream | 1/2 cup | yogurt |
| 1/2 cup | Cool Whip | 1 tsp. | honey |

Whip cream - combine with remainder of ingredients - stir and chill.

Prepare fruits of choice to serve with dip.

To keep fruits from discolouration - sprinkle fruit with lemon juice - toss together.

VARIATION: <u>Cream Cheese Dip</u>

2 tbsp.	chopped nuts - pecans	1-8 oz. pkg.	cream cheese
1 cup	whipping cream	2 tbsp.	lemon juice
1/4 cup	powdered or icing sugar		

Whip cream till stiff - set aside.

Beat together cheese, icing sugar and lemon juice - fold in the whipped cream.

Spread over an assortment of fresh fruit placed in layers, in a clear serving bowl.

Sprinkle nuts on top.

Dry Ribs

1 lb.	pork spareribs	1 tsp.	soya sauce
1/2 cup	water	4 tbsp.	corn starch
1/4 tsp.	5 spice powder *	1/2 tsp.	salt
1/8 tsp.	pepper	1	egg
1/2 tsp.	finely chopped garlic		cooking oil

Cut ribs into small pieces as for sweet and sour ribs.
In a baking dish place the ribs and water - cover with foil.

Bake @ 325° - 60 mins.
Drain excess fat - cool.

In a bowl combine and mix together all other ingredients - except the oil. Pour mixture over the pre-cooked ribs - stir well - let marinate 15 mins. or more.

Heat some oil in a heavy pan - fry ribs in batches till brown and crispy (approx 15 mins.). Watch carefully.

Drain on paper towel - serve with favorite sauces.

* 5 spice powder is available in the specialty section of your local supermarket.

The darkest hour is always when you can't find the light switch.

Why not go out on the limb, that's where the fruit is.

Hot Chocolate

2 sqs.	semi sweet chocolate - chopped
1/3 cup	sugar
4 cups	milk

Melt chopped chocolate in double boiler over hot water.
Add sugar and 1/2 cup of the milk - stir together.

Heat to boiling point **but** DO NOT BOIL - remove from heat.
Add rest of milk - beat with a rotary beater till frothy.

Serve with a dollop of whipped cream or marshmallow.

Hot Chocolate - Cocoa Mix - Dry

10 cups	non-fat milk powder
4 3/4 cups	powdered or icing sugar
1 3/4 cup	cocoa powder
1-6oz. jar	powdered non-dairy cream

Mix together - store in an airtight container = 45 servings.

One Serving = 1/3 cup cocoa dry mix plus 3/4 cup boiling water.
Top with a marshmallow.

Cranberry Sherbet Punch

2 cups	cranberry juice	1-2 litre	bottle Ginger Ale
4 cups	prepared lemonade	1 litre	raspberry sherbet
1 cup	orange juice		

Chill juices till serving time - add chilled Ginger Ale and sherbet - stir
to blend.

Diet pop will make punch more fizzy.

Smith Iced Tea

5	tea bags	1 cup	sugar
5 cups	boiling water		ice cubes (45-50)

Steep tea for 5 mins. - squeeze out and remove bags.
Add sugar - stir to dissolve - add ice cubes to hot tea - stir.

Pour tea into glasses half filled with ice cubes.

Individual servings: use 1 tea bag - 1 cup boiling water - 3 tbsp. sugar and ice.

NOTE: I had to acquire a taste for this when I married as this was a must during the harvest season. Be careful - it can be addictive especially on those hot summer days.

Raspberry - Cranberry Punch

1-3 oz. pkg.	raspberry jello
2 cups	boiling water
1 envelope	raspberry Kool Aid (prepared)
2 cans	frozen lemon concentrate (prepared)
1-2 litre	bottle cranberry juice
1-2 litre	bottle Ginger Ale
2 cups	ice cream - opt.

Pour boiling water over jello - stir to dissolve.
Combine all juices - add to the jello mix - chill.

To serve - add 1-2 litre bottle of Ginger Ale and ice cream.

Milk Shakes

1 pint	ice cream - flavour of choice
1/2- 3/4 cup	milk

Blend together in a blender till smooth. Serve immediately.

VARIATION: Method as above.
Peanut Butter - use vanilla or chocolate ice cream plus 2 tbsp. peanut butter.
Cinnamon Apple - use vanilla ice cream plus 1/2 tsp. cinnamon and small diced apple.
Mocha - use chocolate ice cream plus 2 tsp. instant coffee granules.
Malt - add 2 tbsp. instant malt powder to a basic milk shake.

Orange Julius

1-6 oz.	frozen orange juice concentrate	1 cup	milk
1 cup	water	1/2 cup	sugar
1 tsp.	vanilla	10-12	ice cubes

Blend in blender one minute.

Apple Cider

8 cups	apple juice	1 tsp.	allspice - whole
1/2 cup	brown sugar	1-6"	cinnamon stick
1 tsp.	whole cloves		

In saucepan combine apple juice and sugar.

Tie spices together in a spice bag or cheese cloth - add to apple juice.
Heat to boiling point - reduce heat - cover and simmer 10 mins.
Remove spice bag - serve cider in mugs with floating orange wedges or orange slices studded with a whole clove. = 8 servings.

Solar (Sun) Tea

Fill a large glass container with cold water
Add: 1 tea bag per qt. of water

Place jar in a sunny place with the lid on. Your deck is a perfect place to make your sun tea. Let sit till desired strength.

Wassail (Non-Alcoholic)

1 lge. can	frozen Hawaiian punch	1/2 tbsp.	cloves
1 lge. can	frozen apple juice	1	cinnamon stick

Simmer for about 1/2 hour. Serve hot on a cold night.

Clear Punch

Mix together:	1-2 litre	bottle of 7-Up
	1	bottle of white grape juice

VARIATION: Add apple juice.

Grape Fizz

2 cups	grape juice	3 tbsp.	lemon juice
1 tbsp.	sugar	1 litre	Ginger Ale

Mix together sugar - grape and lemon juice - chill.
Add Ginger Ale when served.

Tropical Punch

6 cups	cold water - divided
2 cups	sugar
5	bananas
1-48 oz. can	pineapple juice
2 cans	frozen orange juice concentrate
2 cans	frozen lemonade concentrate
1-2 litre bottle	lemon lime soda pop

In food processor - blend together bananas - sugar and one cup of the above water.

Combine and mix together all juices with remaining 5 cups of water - add to the banana mixture.

<u>To serve</u> add 1-2 litre bottle of lemon lime soda pop - makes 11 quarts.

Cherry-Orange Kool-Aid Punch

1 pkg.	orange Kool Aid
1 pkg.	cherry Kool Aid
1 cup	sugar - divided
1 env.	orange tang or frozen orange juice
1-48 oz. can	pineapple juice (optional)
1-2 litre	bottle Ginger Ale
	water and ice

Mix Kool Aid using 7 cups water and 1/2 cup sugar per package of Kool Aid.
Mix tang using 2 cups water or frozen orange juice with 2 cans water.
Add pineapple juice. Stir in Ginger Ale and ice just before serving. For more punch use 2 pkgs. more of each flavour Kool Aid - additional sugar and water.

Extra pineapple and Ginger Ale ARE NOT NEEDED.

Sunshine Wedding Punch

2-#5 cans/3 litres	orange juice	juice of 15	lemons
2-#5 cans/3 litres	pineapple juice	10 cups	sugar
15 pkgs.	raspberry Kool Aid	8 cups	water
3 1/2 gallons	water	Ginger Ale	(opt.)

In a large pot mix sugar with 8 cups cold water - bring to a boil. Remove from heat - cool.

Add juices - orange-lemon-pineapple and Kool Aid plus 3 1/2 gallons of water.

Before serving - Ginger Ale may be added and more orange juice.

Challenge for the day......

Life is a song - sing it

Life is a game - play it

Life is a challenge - meet it

Life is a dream - realize it

Life is a sacrifice - offer it

Life is LOVE - enjoy it

Dipped Chocolate Coconut Balls

1/2 cup	butter or margarine	3 cups	chopped pecans
1 can	sweetened	2 cups	flaked coconut
	condensed milk	2 1/2 cups	chocolate chips
6 1/2 cups	powdered sugar	*1/8 lb.	paraffin wax
1 1/2 cup	marachino cherries		
	(drained and chopped)		

* If using candy making chocolate - you may omit wax.

Thoroughly mix together by hand - butter - milk and icing sugar as for pie dough.

Add: cherries - pecans and coconut - combine well - place in fridge till firm. (Overnight if desired.) Roll into balls the size of a cherry.

Melt together chocolate chips and paraffin wax in a double boiler. Using forks - dip balls into the chocolate mixture and place on waxed paper to dry.

Yield 5 lbs. or 150 coconut balls.

Using a teaspoon top balls with left over chocolate to cover imperfections. (Can let it run down sides a bit.)

Nuts and Bolts

5 tbsp.	melted butter	3 cups	Cheerio's
1/2 tsp.	onion salt	3 cups	Bugles
1/2 tsp.	garlic salt	3 cups	Shreddies or Krispix
1/2 tsp.	celery salt	3 cups	pretzel sticks
		2 cups	peanuts

Mix together butter - onion - garlic and celery salts.
Into a large roaster - place remainder of ingredients.
Pour butter mixture over and stir well.
Bake @ 250° - 2 hours - stirring occasionally.
Cool well - store in a tightly covered container.

Turtles

| 1/2 lb. | soft caramels | 1 cup | pecan halves |
| 2 tbsp. | heavy cream or sweetened condensed milk | 4 sqs. | semi-sweet melted chocolate |

In a saucepan over med. heat or microwave melt caramels together with milk.

On a well buttered cookie sheet scatter pecan halves.

With a spoon drop caramel mixture in mounds over pecans. Let stand till firm (approx. 30 mins.)

Melt semi-sweet chocolate and dip each mound in it. Place on wax paper to dry.

Chocolate Almond Brittle

1 cup	butter or margarine	1 tsp.	vanilla
2 1/2 cups	sugar	1 cup	mixed nuts (finely chopped)
1 1/2 cups	unblanched almonds (sliced)	9 oz.	semi-sweet chocolate

In a heavy saucepan melt butter - carefully add sugar - stirring continuously to avoid having the sugar stick to sides of saucepan. Stir till sugar is mixed well with the butter and melted - no crystals left. Remove from heat. Wet a piece of cheese cloth - wrap it around a fork and wipe around sides of saucepan to remove all sugar crystals. Add almonds to the mixture, return to the heat - bring to a 290° temp., (may take 20 mins.). Stir often and continuously near the end of cooking time - remove from heat - stir in vanilla. Pour into a buttered jelly roll pan - spread evenly - let set. Melt chocolate - spread half over the set brittle - sprinkle with half of the nuts. Place a piece of wax paper on the counter - invert pan to remove brittle onto the paper. Spread remaining chocolate and remainder of nuts. Let set - chip into chunks with a knife.

Chocolate Covered Pretzels

In a double boiler, melt down 1 lb. of white chocolate over med. - low heat on your stove.

When the chocolate is melted, dip your pretzel in it - using a tooth pick and lay out on waxed paper.

** Keep a low heat on while you do the pretzels or place the dish of melted chocolate in an electric fry pan which has a little water in it and set on low temp.

Store in a tightly closed container in fridge or a cool place.

VARIATION: You may use dark chocolate.

Oven Caramel Corn

15 cups	popped corn	1/4 cup	light corn syrup
1/2 cup	butter or margarine	1/2 tsp.	salt
1 cup	brown sugar	1/2 tsp.	soda

Divide popped corn between 2 ungreased baking pans, 9x13".

In a saucepan heat butter - sugar - corn syrup and salt, stirring occasionally, until bubbly around edges.
Continue cooking over medium heat for 5 mins.

Remove from heat, stir in soda until foamy.

Pour on popped corn, stirring until corn is well coated.

Bake in 200° oven for 1 hour - stirring every 15 mins.

English Almond Toffee

Heath Bars

2/3 cup	butter	1/4 tsp.	soda
1/2 cup	sugar	1/2 cup	chocolate chips
1/3 cup	water	1/2 cup	chopped pecans
1/2 tsp.	salt	2/3 cup	almonds
			- blanched

Combine in a saucepan - butter - sugar - water and salt.
Stir constantly until it boils.
Cook without stirring until it reaches 236° or until a little dropped into cold water forms a soft ball.

Add almonds - remove from heat.

Mixture will turn a caramel color - stir in soda.

Turn out mixture onto a greased cookie sheet - spread to 1/4" thickness.

Put on chocolate chips - spread as chocolate melts.
Sprinkle with pecans - cool - break into pieces.

To toast almonds or coconut.

Spread on to an ungreased baking sheet - single layer. Toast @ 350° oven till golden color. Shake pan and _watch closely_ - coconut burns easily. Toasting will bring out flavor.

Delicious Microwave Fudge

3/4 cup (1 1/2 sticks)	butter or margarine
3 cups	sugar
1-5 oz. can	evaporated milk (2/3 cup)
2 cups (12 oz)	semi-sweet chocolate chips
1 jar (7 oz)	marshmallow cream
1 1/2 cup	chopped nuts (walnuts or pecans - optional)
1 1/2 tsp.	vanilla

MICROWAVE margarine or butter in a 4 qt. bowl on HIGH for 1 minute or until melted. Add sugar and milk - mix well.

Microwave on HIGH for five minutes or until mixture begins to boil, stirring after 3 mins. Mix well - scrape bowl. Microwave on HIGH 5 1/2 mins. stirring after 3 mins..

Remove from microwave and gradually stir in chocolate chips until melted. Add remaining ingredients - mix well.

Pour into prepared buttered 9x13 pan. Cool at room temperature - cut into squares. Makes 3 lbs.

A batch of this fudge packed into a decorated candy tin - would bring a smile to your hostess.

Poppycock or Popcorn Balls

8 cups	popped corn	1/2 tsp.	vanilla
	(remove unpopped kernels)	2/3 cup	almonds
1 cup	butter or margarine	1 1/3 cup	pecans
1 1/3 cup	sugar		
1/2 cup	white syrup		

Mix together in a bowl - popcorn - pecans and almonds.

In a heavy saucepan over med. heat - melt margarine - add sugar and syrup.
Boil until mixture turns a light caramel colour or at a hard ball stage when tested in water (see below). Remove from heat - stir in the vanilla.

Pour over the popped corn - mix to coat well.
Spread out on a cookie sheet to cool and dry.
Break apart and store in a tightly covered container or plastic ziplock bags.

Makes = 2 lbs.

Popcorn Balls
Substitute 1 cup peanuts and 1 cup of baking gums in place of pecans and almonds.
Form into balls with well buttered hands. Dry on wax paper.

Testing for Hard Ball Stage
Drop approx. 1/2 tsp. of cooked mixture into a cup of cold water.
Pick up candy with fingers and it forms into a soft ball which has lost all plasticity and will roll around on a plate.
Use clean water for each test.

These were great snacks when they showed up at a family reunion.

Notes:

The Weekender

Brunch
Sandwiches
Snacks

French Toast

1/2 cup	butter or margarine	3/4 tsp.	cardamon
1/3 cup	orange juice	5 slices	dry old bread
2 tsps.	grated orange peel		3/4" thick or
4	eggs	10 slices	French Bread

Powdered sugar and pancake syrup.

Place butter into 9x13 glass oven proof dish - in 300° oven to melt - spread evenly.

Remove from oven - increase temp. to 450°.

Combine juice - peel - eggs and cardamon - beat well.

Dip both sides of bread into mixture - place single layer in buttered pan.

Bake @ 450° - 5-6 mins. each side - turning only once when browned.

Sprinkle with powdered sugar - serve with syrup. Serves 3-4.

Ham and Cheese Brunch

9 slices	day old bread - crusts removed - cut into cubes		
1 1/2 lb.	pre-cooked ham-cubed	2 1/2 cups	milk
3/4 cup	grated cheddar cheese	1/2 cup	butter melted
7	eggs	1/4 tsp.	dry mustard

Place bread cubes into a greased 9x13" pan - place ham over bread - sprinkle with cheese.

Beat together eggs - milk - mustard - pour over mixture in pan. Drizzle melted butter over the top - cover with foil.

Refrigerate overnight - bake @ 325° for 1 hour - let stand 5 mins. before serving.

Oma's Potato Pancakes

6	med.-sized potatoes	2	eggs
1 1/2 tsp.	salt	1 cup	flour

Wash - peel and grate potatoes - do not drain.
Place potatoes in a bowl and add eggs - salt and flour - mix together.
If mixture does not have enough moisture and batter is too thick, add
a little water - if to thin add a little more flour.

Lightly brush skillet with oil - use approximately 3 tbsp. batter to
make a 6" pancake - brown on both sides.

Pan may need to be greased between each pancake fried.

Makes approximately 10 pancakes - serve with syrup or sugar.

Oma's Phlinzen - Pancakes

2	eggs	1/2 tsp.	salt
1 tsp.	sugar	1 1/2 cup	milk - sweet/sour
1 tbsp.	oil	1 1/2 cup	flour

In a large bowl beat eggs well - add sugar - oil - salt and milk.
Slowly add flour - beat till smooth - batter should be quite thin.
(Extra milk may be needed.)

Heat 9" non-stick pan - brush lightly with oil for better browning.
Pour 1/3 cup of batter into hot pan - lift and tilt pan to spread batter
over entire surface. Pancake should be about 1/8" thick.

Turn pancake when browned - fry on other side - serve with pancake
syrup. Pancakes may be rolled up like a crepe.

** You may substitute a portion of the milk with thin cream - makes
a richer pancake.

Family tradition is eating leftovers for breakfast the next morning -
with peanut butter and honey- now we use the micro to reheat.

Eggs Benedict with Hollandaise Sauce

Hollandaise Sauce

1/2 cup	butter - room temp. - cut into thirds
1 tbsp.	lemon juice
3	egg yolks - beaten
1 tbsp.	water

dash of pepper
dash of salt

Combine yolks - water - lemon juice - salt and pepper and heat in a heavy saucepan. Add one piece of butter - cook - stirring rapidly until butter has melted and sauce begins to thicken.
Add more butter - one piece at a time - stirring constantly - cook 1-2 mins. Remove from heat immediately.

If sauce is to thick or curdles - immediately add 1-2 tbsp. hot tap water.

Eggs Benedict: Split 3 English Muffins in half - toast and butter.
6 thin slices - cooked ham or fried back bacon.
6 poached eggs.
On each muffin half - place bacon - top with poached egg.
Spoon hollandaise sauce over the top. = 6 servings.

To center yolks in boiled eggs - shake the egg well before cooking.

When poaching eggs - add a teaspoon of vinegar - will keep whites from separating.

Waffles

2 cups	milk	4 tsps.	baking powder
2 cups	flour	1/2 tsp.	salt
2	eggs - separated	1/2 cup	butter - melted

Beat egg whites - set aside. Beat egg yolks thoroughly.
Add milk - flour - baking powder and salt - beat well.
Fold in melted butter and beaten egg whites.

Pour about 1/2 cup of batter onto centre of hot waffle iron -
spreading with a spoon if necessary.

Bake till steaming stops.

VARIATIONS OF TOPPINGS:
Butter and Pancake Syrup
*Sour Cream, Rhubarb Sauce, Cinnamon
Peanut Butter, Sliced Bananas, Maple Syrup
*Sour Cream, Brown Sugar, Blueberries
Whipped Cream, Strawberries/Raspberries and Peaches
Steamed Sweetened Apples or Applesauce
Sunflower Seeds
* Plain yogurt may be used instead of sour cream.

Rhubarb Sauce   Cut washed rhubarb in 1/2" slices - add a little
water. Cover - cook over low heat till soft.

Add sugar to taste (frozen rhubarb needs no water).

Casual entertaining!

*With a waffle iron at each end of the table -
bake these waffles and serve the toppings
suggested.*

A simple meal with a relaxed atmosphere.

Pancakes

2	eggs	1 1/4 cup	buttermilk
1/2 tsp.	soda	1 tsp.	sugar
1 1/4 cup	flour	1/2 tsp.	salt
1 tsp.	baking powder	2 tbsp.	oil

Mix all together until blended.

Drop desired amount of batter on to a hot greased skillet.

Serve with favorite pancake syrup.

Crepes

6	eggs	2/3 cup	butter or margarine
3 tbsp.	sugar	1 1/2 cups	flour
1 tsp.	vanilla	1 1/2 cups	milk
1/4 tsp.	salt		

Beat eggs with mixer - add sugar - salt and vanilla - blend.
Add melted butter - blend in milk and flour - beat till smooth.

Pour 3 tbsp. in greased hot crepe pan - tip pan to swirl batter all over pan bottom.

Turn crepe when underside is lightly browned.
If you want both sides browned - turn just for a few seconds.
Stack with waxed paper between each crepe.
When ready to use - roll crepes - reheat in microwave if necessary - serve with desired topping.

TO SERVE:
Sprinkle with powdered sugar.
Pancake syrup - whipped cream - strawberries - blueberries or apple cinnamon mix.
Apple Cinnamon Mix: Peel and slice or cube apples.
Steam in microwave till fork tender. Mash if desired - add sugar and cinnamon to taste.

43

Chicken a la King

1/4 cup	margarine
1 can	sliced mushrooms - drained
1/2 cup	finely diced green pepper
1/3 cup	flour
1/2 cup	light cream
1 can	cream of chicken soup
1 cup	chicken broth
2 cups	cubed cooked chicken or turkey
1/4 cup	pimento
8	toast cups

In a skillet - stir and cook together margarine - mushrooms and peppers.
Stir in flour - add cream - soup and chicken broth.
Cook till thickened - add chicken and pimento - heat through until hot.

Spoon into prepared toast cups = serves 4.

Toast Cups: Prepare using thin sliced fresh bread.
Remove crusts - spread bread with soft butter.
Press bread - buttered side down in muffin cups.
Bake @ 375° - 12 mins. or till lightly toasted.

Tuna Filling:
1 can mushroom soup
2 small cans flaked tuna - drained
2 green onions - sliced fine
Mix together - spoon into toast cups - place under broiler oven till bubbling.

Use your leftover chicken or turkey.

Make the Chicken a la King in advance - freeze the filling - use when the occasion calls for it.

Omelet - Plain

4	eggs
1 1/2 tbsp.	cold water
	salt and pepper
2 tbsp.	butter

In a bowl place eggs - water - salt and pepper.
Using fork - beat only till combined.

In a skillet - heat butter tilting pan to coat all sides. Add egg mixture - cook over medium heat. As eggs set - run spatula around edge of pan lifting and letting uncooked portion flow underneath. When eggs are set but still shiny - remove pan from heat. Fold omelet in half.

VARIATIONS:
Grated Cheddar Cheese
Sliced Mushrooms
Diced Ham
Sliced Green Pepper

Add any or all of these to enhance your omelet. Place on omelet before folding in half. Cook a little longer.

Elyce's Coffee Cake

Sunday A.M. Brunch

1/2 cup	margarine	1 pkg.	yeast
1/2 cup	hot water	1 1/2 cup	flour - divided
2 tbsp.	sugar	1	egg yolk
1 tsp.	salt		

Melt margarine in a bowl - add hot water - sugar - salt - yeast and 1/2 cup flour. Beat 2 mins..
Add egg yolk and beat 1 min. longer. Stir in about 1 cup flour to make a stiff enough dough to handle.

Cover with plastic wrap - refrigerate 2 hrs or overnight.

In morning prepare: **Topping Mix**

1/4 cup	**sugar**
1 1/2 tsp.	**cinnamon**
1 cup	**chopped walnuts**

Press out dough on a floured surface to 8x10" size.
Sprinkle with half of topping mix - fold over and press out dough again to an 8x10" size. Spread on remainder of mix - fold over and press out again to an 8x10" size. Place on greased baking sheet - bake @ 400° 15 - 20 mins. Watch so it does not burn. Frost with icing.

NOTE: This can be mixed up Saturday night and is great served for Sunday A.M. brunch.

People who say it cannot be done, should not interrupt those who are doing it.

Sandwich Fillings

Some fillings are suitable for regular sandwiches...others are used for ribbon or rolled sandwiches.

To make ribbon or rolled sandwiches - use large sandwich loaves that have been sliced lengthwise with crusts removed.

Wrap filled sandwiches in plastic wrap - refrigerate overnight if possible - cut into desired thickness for serving.

Egg Salad Filling:
4	hard boiled eggs - chopped
2 tbsp.	chopped green onion or grated onion
	salt and pepper to taste
2-4 tbsp.	salad dressing
1 tsp.	prepared mustard (opt.)

Combine and mix thoroughly.

Ham Filling:
1 lb.	ham - minced - chopped (meat of choice)
Add:	chopped dill pickles or green relish
Add:	salad dressing for spreading consistency

Cream Cheese Filling:
Cream:	1 /2 lb. cream cheese (may add some food coloring)
Add:	salad dressing for spreading consistency
Garnish:	use chopped red and green maraschino cherries.

VARIATIONS:

Flaked chicken - celery - salad dressing.

Canned salmon - salad dressing - grated onion.

Canned tuna - chopped celery - grated onion - salad dressing.
 (If used for rolled sandwiches - centre with a dill pickle.

Peanut butter for rolled sandwich - centre with a banana.

Cheese Whiz for rolled sandwiches - centre with olives or gherkins.

Bacon Egg on a Muffin

6	eggs beaten	1/2 cup	swiss cheese - shredded
1/3 cup	milk	4 slices	bacon cooked - crumbled
1 tbsp.	Dijon mustard	2 tbsp.	grated parmesan cheese
1/8 tsp.	pepper	1 med.	tomato cut in wedges
3	English muffins split and toasted		alfalfa sprouts (opt.)

Combine eggs - milk - mustard and pepper. Place in a dish to
microwave - on high heat - uncovered 4 - 6 mins..
At intervals stir - moving cooked portions to centre of dish.
Stir in swiss cheese and bacon - cook another 1 - 2 mins. till
cheese is melted BUT eggs should still be moist.

Prepare muffins - split and toast - place on 3 serving plates.
Top each with egg mixture - sprinkle with parmesan cheese -
serve with tomato wedges and alfalfa sprouts.

Bacon Cheese Broiler Buns

4	Kaiser rolls - split
4	slices bacon - not to crisp - micro or fry - cut in half
	Cheese Whiz
	tomato slices

Place Kaiser rolls on a cookie sheet - cut side up.
Spread with cheese whiz - top with bacon and a tomato slice - put
in oven under broiler.

Broil till bacon is crisp - cheese bubbles and is brown.

Nacho's

nacho chips
grated cheddar cheese
sour cream

green onions - chopped
diced tomatoes
salsa sauce

Pre-heat oven to 350° - spread desired amount of nacho's on cookie sheet. Sprinkle cheddar cheese over and bake till cheese is melted.

Remove from oven - carefully place on a platter with a spatula. Cover with diced tomatoes and onions - serve with sour cream and salsa.

Garlic Bread

1   French loaf - cut into 3/4" slices
Cut thro - only partially so bread remains attached at bottom.
Spread the following mixture between slices.

1 mashed garlic clove - 1/2 cup soft butter.
Wrap in foil - place on a baking sheet.

Bake @ 400° - 15-20 mins.

VARIATION:

Cut loaf through lengthwise.

Mix together - 2 minced garlic cloves with 2 tsp. olive oil.

Spread on each half and sprinkle over top a mixture of:

1 tbsp. parsley   1 tsp. paprika   1 tsp. marjoram
1 tbsp. thyme   2 tbsp. parmesan cheese

Wrap in foil - place on baking sheet - bake @ 400° - 15 -20 mins.
To brown - place under broiler - serve immediately.

Grilled Patti Melt on Rye

Rye bread slices
sauteed onions
cheese slices

fried hamburger patties
Thousand Island dressing
butter

Place all above ingredients on rye bread using two slices as for a sandwich.
Butter outside of bread slices - place in a hot skillet.
Brown on both sides as for a grilled cheese sandwich.
NOTE: Hamburger and onions need to be hot when placed on rye bread.

Tuna Ring

1	**loaf frozen bread dough - thawed - softened.**		
	Roll into a rectangle shape - 16x10"		
2-7 oz. cans	**tuna - drained - flake with a fork**		
1/2 cup	**chopped onion**	**1 tsp.**	**celery salt**
1/2 cup	**grated cheddar cheese**	**1/2 tsp.**	**salt**
1	**egg slightly beaten**	**1/4 tsp.**	**pepper**
	(reserve 2 tbsp.)		
1/4 cup	**chopped parsley or 2 tbsp. dried**		

Mix together all ingredients - spread onto rolled dough to within 1" of edge - roll up as you would for cinnamon rolls.

Stretch out dough to give you length as you place a formed circle on a greased cookie sheet or pizza pan - pinch ends together. Leave a 6" circle in centre if possible - using a scissors cut 2/3 of the way thro - the ring making 12 equal sections.
Turn each piece partially on its side - exposing the filling.

Brush the entire ring with reserve egg. Cover let rise till double in size. Bake @ 375° - 30 mins. or till done - serve warm.

To serve fill centre hole with fresh cut tomato wedges - garnish with parsley.

Focaccia Bread

1	loaf Focaccia bread (bakery bought)
	favorite sandwich filling - chicken - tuna - etc.

Slice top half off loaf.
Spread filling on bottom half - replace top.
Wrap loaf in foil.
Place in pre-heated 325° oven - for 20 mins..
*To serve - slice into wedges.
NOTE: Focaccia bread may be used with a dip. Equal
amounts of balsamic vinegar and olivie oil. Sprinkled with fresh
ground pepper. Serve as an appetizer.
* Bread may be pre-heated - before filling is put on - saves time.

Bruchetta

6	fresh tomatoes (diced)	1 tbsp.	minced garlic
1 tbsp.	chopped green onion	1/2 tsp.	lemon juice
1/2 cup	fresh basil leaves	1/2 cup	olive oil
1-2	garlic cloves	salt and pepper to taste	
6	thick slices of French bread or bread of choice		

Toss together tomatoes - minced garlic and onions along with
coarsely chopped basil - lemon juice - salt and pepper.
Add half the oil - set aside.

Heat remainder of oil in a pan - add cloves of garlic - saute 2-3
mins.
Remove garlic cloves from pan.

Toast bread slices - cut in half - arrange on a plate and brush with
garlic flavored oil. Spoon tomato mixture on - serve immediately.

Serves 6

Tuna Melt

2	hamburger buns (split in half)	1 tsp.	lemon juice
1-7oz. tin	flaked tuna - drained	2 tbsp.	onion (minced)
1/3 cup	grated cheddar cheese	1/2 cup	celery (chopped)
1/4 cup	salad dressing	1/4 tsp.	salt
	tomato slices (topping)	1/4 tsp.	pepper

Mix together all ingredients - place filling on bun halves.
Place on baking sheet - under broiler - 3 -5 mins. till hot and
cheese melted. Top each bun with tomato slice when served.

VARIATION:
Pickle relish or hard boiled egg may be added to filling.

Quiche

1-9"	chilled unbaked pie shell	1 1/2 cups	evaporated milk
1/2 lb.	bacon (cut into 1/2" pieces)	2 tbsp.	minced onion
1/2 lb.	shredded swiss cheese	1 tsp.	salt
3	eggs slightly beaten	1/4 cup	parmesan grated cheese
	dash of dried parsley		

Prick bottom and sides of shell with fork - bake @ 425°-10 - 12
mins. Fry bacon till crisp - dry on paper towel - sprinkle bacon
over crust and cheese over bacon.
Stir together eggs - milk - onion and salt - pour into shell.
Sprinkle with parmesan cheese and parsley.
Bake @ 325° - 45 mins. or until pie is golden and centre is firm.
Let stand 10 mins. before serving. Serves 4.

VARIATION: Mini Quiche (approx. 36)
If making tarts more pie pastry will be needed.
Bake in muffin tins - USE AS APPETIZERS
Pre-bake shells @ 425° for 4 mins. - pour in filling.
Bake @ 325° - approx. 25 - 27 mins. - make these ahead - cool -
freeze.
When serving, place on a cookie sheet and heat in the oven.

Parmesan Cheese Bread

Thaw	2 - 1 lb.	loaves frozen bread dough
	1/3 cup	melted butter
	3/4 cup	grated parmesan cheese

Slice each loaf into 6 slices (total 12)
Roll each slice in butter - roll in cheese.
Place pieces slightly overlapping each other into a greased bundt pan. Cover and let rise in a warm place till double in size.

Bake @ 350° for 30 - 40 mins. - till golden brown.
Turn out on a wire rack to cool. Use as a snack or with a casserole dish.

Quesadillas

In a lightly oiled fry pan place a tortilla shell.
Spread with salsa - top with shredded cheddar cheese - place another tortilla on top. When browned - turn over on other side.
Remove from pan - cut into wedges.
Serve with sour cream and salsa

VARIATION:
Cut chicken breast into thin slices.
Brown in an oiled pan adding salt and pepper.
Place cooked chicken over salsa and cheese, spinkle with a little more cheese before putting top tortilla shell on and baking.

Gourmet French Bread Topping

1 cup	mayonnaise (not Miracle Whip)
1/2 cup	parmesan cheese
1 tsp.	worcestershire sauce
	chopped parsley
	paprika

Slice a loaf of French bread lengthwise.
Combine the ingredients - spread the mix on top of bread -
sprinkle with paprika.
Put under broiler until bubbly and brown.
Cut into serving size pieces.

French Bread - see The Bakery.

Notes:

The Bakery

Cakes

Cookies

Bars - Squares

Pies - Tarts

Biscuits

Muffins

Loaves

Yeast Breads

Lazy Daisy Oatmeal Cake

1 1/4 cup	boiling water	2	eggs
1 cup	oatmeal	1 1/2 cups	flour
1/2 cup	margarine	1 tsp.	soda
1 cup	white sugar	1/2 tsp.	salt
1 cup	brown sugar	3/4 tsp.	cinnamon
1 tsp.	vanilla	1/4 tsp.	nutmeg

Pour water over oatmeal - cover - let stand for 20 mins.
Cream together margarine and sugars - add vanilla and eggs -
stir in oatmeal. Mix together flour - soda - salt and spices.
Add to the creamed mixture - mix well - pour into greased 9x13"
pan. Bake @ 350° - 30 -40 mins. - remove from oven - prepare
topping.

1/4 cup	melted margarine	1/3 cup	chopped nuts
1 cup	brown sugar	3/4 cup	coconut
3 tbsp.	cream		

Mix together - put on top of cake - return to oven under broiler till
bubbly.

Rhubarb Cake

2 cups	flour	1 tsp.	baking powder
1/2 cup	butter	1	egg beaten

Mix together with a fork or pastry blender - reserve 1 cup for
topping. Press mixture into an 9x9" pan.

Filling:	4 cups	chopped rhubarb	1/2 cup	flour
	1 1/2 cups	sugar	3 tbsp.	sugar
	1/2 cup	margarine - melted	1 tsp.	cinnamon
	2	eggs - beaten		

Mix together all ingredients except cinnamon and sugar.
Top with reserved crumbs - sugar and cinnamon (mix together).
Bake @ 350° - 1 hour.
Optional - Fresh plums may be used.

Lovelight Chiffon

This cake can be made into a white or chocolate cake.

White Cake		Chocolate Cake
2	eggs (separated)	2
1 1/4 cup	sugar - divided	1 1/2 cup
1 3/4 cup	flour	1 3/4 cup
3 tsp.	baking powder	2 tsp.
1/2 tsp.	salt	1/2 tsp.
nil	soda	3/4 tsp.
nil	cocoa	1/3 cup
1/4 cup - scant	oil	1/4 cup
1 cup (sweet)	milk	1 cup (sour)
1 tsp.	vanilla	1 tsp.

Beat egg whites gradually adding 1/2 cup of the sugar called for.
Continue beating till glossy and in peaks - set aside.

Place dry ingredients in mixing bowl - make a well in centre.
Add egg yolks - oil - vanilla and milk - beat till smooth.
Fold in the beaten egg whites.

Spread into greased 9x13" pan or 2 round 9" layer pans.
Bake @ 325° - 30 - 35 mins.

This cake has been used for a variety of occasions. Showers - Weddings - Birthdays.
Layer cakes with favorite fillings - frosted cupcakes and strawberry shortcake base.

Springtime Sponge Cake

1 1/2 cups	flour	2 tsp.	vanilla
1/4 tsp.	salt	6	eggs - separated
1 tsp.	baking powder	1 1/2 cups	sugar
1/3 cup	cold water	1 tsp.	cream of tartar
1/2 tsp.	almond extract		

Sift together flour - salt - baking powder - set aside.

Measure liquids - water - almond and vanilla extract - set aside.

In mixer bowl beat 6 egg yolks - gradually adding the sugar till thick and lemon coloured. Add liquids alternately with flour mixture - set aside.

In a clean mixer bowl beat 6 egg whites together with cream of tartar till stiff.
Gently fold egg whites into egg yolk mixture.

Pour batter into a 10 inch ungreased tube pan - bake @ 325° - 1 hour.

To cool - invert pan for an hour. Loosen sides of the cake with knife before removing cake.

Delicious served with strawberries and ice cream or your favorite icing.

VARIATIONS:

Orange Sponge - Add 1 tbsp. orange zest.
Substitute - orange juice in place of water *omit* - almond extract.

Chocolate Sponge - **Add** 1/3 cup cocoa powder - *omit* - almond extract.

Raisin Cake

Prepare raisins: 2 cups raisins - cover with 4 cups water - simmer 20 mins.. Drain well - reserve 1 cup liquid.

1 cup	butter - scant	2 tsp.	soda
1 1/2 cups	brown sugar	1/2 tsp.	nutmeg
2	eggs	1 tsp.	cinnamon
3 cups	flour - divided	1 cup	milk
1/2 tsp.	salt	1 cup	reserved liquid
1/2 tsp.	cloves		

Dust and dredge drained raisins with one cup of above flour portion.
Cream together - butter - sugar and eggs.
Sift together all dry ingredients - add to the creamed mix alternately with liquids.
Stir in the dredged raisins.

Pour into a greased 9x13" pan - bake @ 350° for 35 - 40 mins.
Frost with caramel icing.

Carrot Cake

2 cups	flour	1 1/4 cup	oil
1 3/4 cup	sugar	2 tsp.	vanilla
2 tsp.	soda	1/2 cup	orange juice
1 tsp.	salt	2 cups	grated carrots
2 tsp.	cinnamon	3/4 cup	coconut
3	eggs lightly beaten	3/4 cup	chopped nuts
		1/2 cup	raisins (opt.)

Stir together dry ingredients - combine eggs - oil - vanilla and juice.
Add to dry mix - beat 3 mins. on low speed - stir in the carrots - coconut and nuts. Pour into a greased 9x13" pan.
Bake @ 325° - 45 - 55 mins. Ice with cream cheese icing - sprinkle with chopped pecans and coconut.
* This has been served many times as a wedding cake.

Popcorn Cake

30 cups	popped popcorn (remove unpopped kernels)
1 cup	baking gums (ju-jubes or gummy bears)
1 cup	salted peanuts
1/2 cup	smarties - optional
1/2 cup	oil
1/2 cup	margarine or butter
1 1/2 tsp.	salt
2 pkgs.	marshmallows (regular size - 800 g)

In a large bowl combine and mix popcorn - candy - peanuts and smarties.

In a saucepan over low heat stir together oil - margarine - salt and marshmallows.
Heat until well blended - pour over popcorn - stir till coated and combined.

Pack firmly into a greased tube pan (angel food cake pan) or a 9x13" pan.

This mixture may be shaped into balls.

Puffed Wheat Cake

1/2 cup	butter	3 tbsp.	cocoa
1 cup	brown sugar	2 tsp.	vanilla
1/2 cup	corn syrup	9 cups	puffed wheat

In a saucepan stir together butter - syrup - sugar and cocoa.
Bring to a full boil - boil 1 min. - remove from heat.
Stir in vanilla and puffed wheat - coat well.

Press into a buttered 9x13" pan - chill - cut into squares.

Poppy Seed Cake

1/2 cup	poppy seeds	2 cups	flour
1 cup	milk	2 tsp.	baking powder
3/4 cup	margarine	1/2 tsp.	salt
1 1/2 cup	sugar	4	eggs
1 tsp.	vanilla		(separated)

Combine poppy seeds and milk - soak for 1 hour at room temperature.

Cream together margarine and sugar - add vanilla.
Combine together flour - baking powder - salt - add alternately to the creamed mixture with milk and poppy seed mix.

Beat the egg whites until very stiff - fold into the above gently, but combine well.
Pour into 3 layer cake pans which are well greased and floured.

Bake @ 350° - 35 - 40 mins. - Cool for 10 mins. - invert on cake rack.
Cool completely.

Filling:

4	egg yolks	1 1/2 cups	milk
3/4 cup	sugar	1/2 cup	chopped nuts
2 tbsp.	corn starch	1 tsp.	vanilla
1/4 tsp.	salt		

In a heavy saucepan - combine milk - egg yolks - sugar - corn starch and salt. Cook for 5 mins. - stirring constantly - remove from heat.
Stir in vanilla and nuts - cool - spread between cake layers.

Frosting:

1/2 cup	butter or margarine
1 1/2 cups	powdered or icing sugar
1 tsp.	vanilla
2 tbsp.	cocoa
	cold coffee

Combine dry ingredients with enough coffee to make icing the right consistency for spreading - stir in vanilla. Beat well.
Frost top and sides of cake.

Black Forest Cake

1 cup	butter	3 cups	flour
2 cups	brown sugar	1/3 cup	cocoa
4	eggs	4 tsp.	baking powder
2 tbsp.	corn syrup	2 tsp.	soda
2 tsp.	vanilla	1/4 tsp.	salt
2 cups	cold water	2 tbsp.	vinegar

Combine dry ingredients - flour - cocoa - baking powder - soda and salt - set aside.

In mixing bowl cream butter - add sugar - eggs - syrup and vanilla, beat well. Add dry ingredients to the creamed mixture alternately with combined liquids of water and vinegar - beat well.

Put in to a greased and floured 9x13" pan - bake @ 350° - 40 - 45 mins.

Remove cake from oven - let stand 5 mins. - loosen sides with a knife blade. Invert on a cooling rack.

Filling and Frosting:

1-21 oz. can	cherry pie filling
1/2 tsp.	vanilla
20	maraschino cherries - drained
3 cups	whipping cream
2 sqs.	semi-sweet chocolate
	powdered or icing sugar to sweeten cream

Place cooled cake on a large serving tray- split cake in two layers. Whip the cream - adding vanilla and icing sugar to sweeten. On bottom layer spread cherry pie filling - top with a portion of whipped cream.

Place top cake layer on cream - frost top and sides with more cream. Use some of the cream in a cake decorator tube to make dollops around the edge and centre of cake - place a cherry in the centre of each dollop.

To Make Chocolate Curls: For top of cake.
Semi-sweet chocolate squares need to be at room temperature. Shave off thin slices using a sharp knife or vegetable peeler.

Apricot Crumble Cake

1-8 oz. pkg.	cream cheese	2 cups	flour
1/2 cup	margarine	1 tsp.	baking powder
1 1/4 cup	sugar	1/2 tsp.	soda
2	eggs	1/4 tsp.	salt
1/4 cup	milk	1-12 oz.	apricot preserves
1 tsp.	vanilla		

Blend cream cheese - margarine and sugar - gradually add eggs - milk and vanilla.
Combine dry ingredients - add and mix until well blended.

Pour half the batter into greased and floured 9x13" pan - cover with apricots.
Top with other half of batter - bake @ 350° - 35 - 40 mins.

Combine	2 cups	coconut	1 tsp.	cinnamon
	2/3 cup	brown sugar	1/3 cup	melted butter

Spread over cake - place under broiler till golden brown.

* **Watch** so this does not burn on you !!!!!

One Bowl Chocolate Cake

1 3/4 cup	flour	1/2 cup	oil
1 1/2 cup	sugar	2	eggs
1 1/2 tsp.	baking soda	1 tsp.	vanilla
1/2 tsp.	salt	1 1/2 cup	milk - sweet/sour
1/2 cup	cocoa	1 tbsp.	vinegar

Place dry ingredients in bowl - make a well in centre.
Add the rest of ingredients - blend together and beat 3 mins.

Pour into a greased 9x13" pan - bake @ 350° - 30 - 35 mins.

NOTE: This recipe will make 24 cup cakes - bake 20 mins..

Oma's Crumb Cake

3/4 cup	butter	1 tsp.	baking soda
1 cup	sugar	1/4 tsp.	cloves
2 cups	flour	1/4 tsp.	nutmeg
1	egg	1/2 tsp.	cinnamon
1 cup	sour milk		

Cream butter till soft and creamy - add in sugar gradually.
Beat till light and fluffy.

Using a fork blend in flour to make a coarse corn meal mix -
reserve 1 cup for top of cake.

Add baking soda and spices.
Beat egg till foamy, add milk and continue to beat, till blended.
Add the dry crumb mix - stir till smooth but do not over mix.

Spread batter into a greased 9" square pan - sprinkle reserved
crumbs on top.
Press lightly into batter.

Bake @ 350° - 30 - 35 mins.

VARIATION: Add 1 cup chopped raisins to batter.

If I really cared:

I would look you in the eyes - when you talk
to me.

I would think about what you are saying -
rather than what I am going to say next.

I would hear your feelings - as well as your
words.

Spiced Coffee Cake

1/2 cup	margarine	1 1/2 cups	flour
1 cup	brown sugar	1/2 tsp.	soda
1	egg	1 tsp.	vanilla
	pinch of salt	1/2 tsp.	cinnamon
3/4 cup	sour milk	1 tsp.	baking powder
1/2 cup	raisins	1/4 tsp. ea.	cloves and nutmeg

Cream together margarine and sugar - add egg and vanilla - stir.
Mix dry ingredients together - add alternately with milk to the above.
Add raisins which are dusted lightly with a little flour.

Spread into a greased 9" square pan - prepare topping.

Topping: 1/3 cup   chopped nuts
               1/3 cup   brown sugar
Combine and sprinkle over batter in pan.
Bake @ 350° - 25 mins.

66

Light Fruitcake

4 lbs.	raisins		4 cups	flour - divided
2 lbs.	glazed cherries		1 lb.	butter
1 lb.	mixed fruit		2 cups	sugar
1/2 lb.	walnuts		12	eggs
1/2 cup	sliced almonds		2 tsp.	flavoring
3/4cup	brazil nuts - halves		1 tsp.	soda
3/4 cup	filberts		1 tsp.	salt
1/2 cup	fruit juice			

Wash raisins and blanch with boiling water - 2 mins. - drain.
Dry well with paper towels.
Mix together all fruits and nuts with one cup of the flour.

Cream together butter and sugar - add eggs one at a time beating
well after each addition.
Mix together dry ingredients - add to creamed mixture alternately
with fruit juice and flavouring ending with flour mix.
Stir in fruit and nut mixture.

Prepare 4-5 loaf pans with double lined brown paper and greased
well.
Bake @ 275° for 2 1/2 - 3 hrs. - placing a pan of water on lowest
rack for moisture.

Let stand in pans till cool - remove paper and re-wrap in foil for
storage or freezing.

NOTE: Fruit cake needs time to ripen and fruit flavors to blend.

For a darker cake use juices such as plum, cranberry, raspberry.

For a lighter cake use pineapple juice.

Gumdrop Fruit Cake

4 cups	light raisins	1 1/2 cups	butter
2 cups	gumdrops	1 1 /2 cups	sugar
1 cup	almonds	6	eggs
3 cups	flour - divided	1/2 cup	light cream
1 tsp.	baking powder	1 tbsp.	lemon juice
1/4 tsp.	salt		

Blanch raisins in boiling water 2 mins. - drain well - pat dry with towel.
Combine gumdrops - raisins and almonds - dust with one cup of the flour.

In mixer bowl cream together butter and sugar - cream well.
Add eggs - one at a time - beating well after each addition.
Mix together the remainder of flour - baking powder and salt.
Stir in to the creamed mixture adding alternately with liquids.
Blend in gumdrops and nut mixture.

Line 3 loaf pans with double layers of brown paper - grease well - spoon in batter.

Bake @ 250° for 2 1/2 hrs. or till well cooked.

VARIATION: Mixed fruit and cherries may be used in place of gumdrops.

This cake makes us think of Christmas.
To frost window panes dissolve epsom salts in beer and apply with a brush.

Ebea's Chocolate Chip Cookies

1 cup	margarine	1 tsp.	vanilla
1/8 cup	butter	3 cups	flour
3/4 cup	brown sugar	1 tsp.	salt
3/4 cup	white sugar	1 tsp.	soda
2	eggs	2 cups	chocolate chips
2 tbsp.	corn syrup		

Cream together - margarine - butter - sugars - eggs - syrup and vanilla. Combine flour - soda and salt - add to the creamed mixture -beat well. Stir in chocolate chips.

With a teaspoon drop mounds of dough on an ungreased baking sheet.

Bake @ 325° for 13 - 15 mins.
Allow to cool on baking sheet for one min. before removing to rack.
Yields - 4 Dozen

Oatmeal Raisin Cookies

3/4 cup	margarine	1	egg
1 1/4 cup	flour (divided)	1 tsp.	baking powder
1 cup	brown sugar	1 tsp.	vanilla
1/4 cup	white sugar	1/4 tsp.	soda
1 1/2 cups	oatmeal	1 cup	raisins
1/8 tsp.	each cloves / cinnamon (opt.)		

Blend oatmeal in a food processor until semi-fine blend.
In a mixing bowl beat margarine for 1 min. - add 3/4 cup flour together with sugars - egg - baking powder - soda and vanilla.
Beat till thoroughly combined - beat in remaining 1/2 cup flour - stir in oatmeal and raisins.
Drop with a teaspoon onto an ungreased baking sheet - 2" apart.
Bake @ 350° - 12 - 14 mins. Allow to cool on baking sheet for 1 min. before removing to rack.
* Chocolate chips may be added instead of raisins.   Makes 36

Marshmallow Caramel Balls

6	caramel toffee bars (McIntosh)	Rice Krispies
1 can	sweetened condensed milk	large marshmallows
2/3 cup butter		coconut

In saucepan - over medium heat - place broken toffee bars add butter and condensed milk - heat till melted and combined. Remove from heat.

Dip marshmallows in sauce - roll in Krispies or coconut.

NOTE: If sauce cools and begins to thicken - set pot into some shallow water in electric fry pan (low heat).
These marshmallow balls freeze well.

Neopolatin Cookies

2 1/4 cups	flour	3/4 cups	sugar
1/2 tsp.	baking powder	1	egg
1/8 tsp.	salt	1 tsp.	vanilla
1 cup	butter or margarine		
1/4 cup	of each red and green cherries		
	red and green food coloring		

Combine flour - baking powder - salt - stir to blend.
In mixer bowl - cream together - butter - sugar - egg and vanilla.
Gradually add dry ingredients - mixing well after each addition.

Divide dough into three equal portions - set one portion aside for plain layer. Add red cherries and red food coloring to second portion - green cherries and green food coloring to the remaining portion. Chill dough for 1 hour.
Shape each portion into a 12x2x1/2" rectangle.
Place layers on top of each other with pink as middle layer.
Chill till firm enough to slice into 1/8" slices.
Place slices on an ungreased baking sheet.
Bake @ 350° - 10 - 12 mins. - cool before removing from pan.
Makes = 5 dozen.

Sugar Cookies

1 cup	margarine	2 1/2 cups	flour
1 cup	sugar	1/2 tsp.	soda
2	eggs - well beaten	2 tsp.	cream of tartar
1 tsp.	vanilla	1/8 tsp.	nutmeg
	pinch of salt		

Cream together margarine and sugar.
Add eggs and vanilla - beat well.
Combine dry ingredients - stir into the creamed mix.

Roll out on floured board approx. 1/4" thickness.
Cut into desired shapes - bake @ 350° - 8 - 10 mins..

Brush on a thin coat of icing - decorate as desired.

Jam-Jam Cookies

1 cup	shortening or margarine	2	eggs
1 cup	brown sugar	2 tsp.	baking soda
1/3 cup	corn syrup or honey	1/4 tsp.	salt
1 tsp.	vanilla	3 1/2 cups	flour

Cream together shortening - sugar and eggs - add syrup and
vanilla. Combine dry ingredients - flour - baking soda and salt.
Stir into the shortening mixture. Dough should be soft but not
sticky. Chill before rolling dough.

On a lightly floured board - roll dough to 1/8" thickness.
Cut into shapes with a round 2 1/2" cookie cutter.
Place on an ungreased cookie sheet.

Bake 350° for 9 - 10 mins. or lightly browned.
Place on a rack to cool. Spread your favourite jam on bottom side
of cookie - then top with another.

NOTE: These cookies freeze well - and will soften, especially
after freezing.

Oatmeal - Date Filled Cookies

1/2 cup	margarine	2 cups	flour
1/2 cup	lard	1 tsp.	baking powder
1 1/2 cup	brown sugar - packed	1 tsp.	soda
2	eggs	1/2 tsp.	salt
1 tsp.	vanilla	3 cups	oatmeal

Cream together margarine and lard - add sugar.
Beat in eggs one at a a time - add vanilla.
Blend flour - baking powder - soda and salt.
Add to creamed mixture - stir well - add oatmeal.

Chill one hour - roll out dough on a floured board to 1/4" thickness.

Cut into shapes with a 2 1/2" cookie cutter.
Place on baking sheet.

Bake @ 350° - 10 - 12 mins. Remove cookies to rack to cool.

Sandwich cookies with date filling.

Date Filling:

2 cups	chopped dates	1/4 cup	brown sugar
1 cup	water	1/4 cup	orange juice

Place into saucepan - cook together for approximately 10 mins. till thickened.
Cool and spread between cookies.

For rolled cookies chill dough for about 1/2 hour. Dough will be easier to handle and require less flour, therefore will make a more tender cookie.

Molasses Cookies

These cookies make excellent gingerbread people.

1 cup	margarine	1 cup	brown sugar
2	eggs	3/4 cup	molasses
2 tsp.	ginger	3/4 cup	milk (sweet/sour)
1 tsp.	cinnamon	1/4 tsp.	salt
1/2 tsp.	nutmeg	1 tsp.	baking soda
4 1/4 cups	flour	2 tsp.	baking powder
1 tsp.	vanilla		

Cream together thoroughly, margarine - sugar - eggs and vanilla.
Combine dry ingredients - add to creamed mixture together with
milk and molasses.
Chill dough.

Roll out dough on a floured board to a 1/4" thickness.
Make cut outs with gingerbread cookie cutter - place on a baking
sheet.
Bake @ 350° for 12 - 15 mins.
Decorate with icing to make gingerbread people.

Gingersnaps

3/4 cup	margarine	1 tsp.	ginger
1 3/4 cup	sugar	1 tsp.	cinnamon
2	eggs	1/2 tsp.	baking powder
1/2 cup	molasses	2 tsp.	soda
1 tsp.	vanilla	1/2 tsp.	salt
4 cups	flour	1/2 tsp.	nutmeg

Cream together till light and fluffy - margarine and sugar.
Add eggs - molasses and vanilla. Combine dry ingredients add to
the creamed mixture. Chill dough for half an hour.
Roll dough into balls - approximately size of a walnut - roll in
sugar.
Place on a greased baking sheet - press down each ball with the
bottom of a tumbler.
Bake @ 350° - 10 - 12 mins.

Peanut Butter Blossoms

1/2 cup	margarine or butter	1	egg
1/2 cup	peanut butter	1 1/4 cups	flour - divided
1/2 cup	white sugar	1/2 tsp.	baking powder
1/2 cup	brown sugar - packed	1/2 tsp.	soda
	or 1/4 cup honey	1/2 tsp.	vanilla

Cream together margarine and peanut butter in mixer.
Add 1/2 cup of the flour -sugars - egg - soda - baking powder and vanilla.
Beat till thoroughly combined - beat in remaining flour.

Cover and chill dough till easy to handle.
Shape into one inch balls - roll in sugar.

Place 2" apart on ungreased baking sheet.
Make a criss-cross design and flatten with tines of fork - dipped in flour.

Bake @ 375° - 7 - 9 mins. or till bottoms lightly browned.

VARIATIONS: Chocolate Kiss Blossoms

Prepare as above but do not flatten with a fork.
After baking immediately top each cookie with a candy kiss.
Press down firmly so cookie cracks around edge.

Date Balls

1 tbsp.	butter	1 1/2 cups	chopped dates
1 cup	sugar	3 cups	Rice Krispies
2	eggs - well beaten		(may need extra)
1 tsp.	vanilla		flaked coconut

In a heavy skillet on stove (med. heat) melt butter.
Add dates - sugar and beaten eggs - heat till it thickens.
Stir in vanilla and Krispies - remove from heat.
Cool slightly - shape into balls - roll in coconut.

Chipnut Choodles

1 cup	chocolate chips
1 cup	butterscotch chips
1 cup	salted peanuts
2/3 cup	dried chow mein noodles

Melt chips in a heavy saucepan over low heat.
Toss in peanuts and noodles and stir till coated.
Drop by small teaspoonfuls on to waxed paper and cool.

Makes = 3 dozen.

Maple Puffs

1 cup	brown sugar	1 3/4 cup	flour
2	eggs	1 1/2 tsp.	baking powder
1/2 tsp.	vanilla	1/2 tsp.	soda
1/2 tsp.	maple flavoring	1/4 tsp.	salt
1 cup	sour cream		

Beat sugar and eggs till blended - add flavorings.
Combine dry ingredients together - add to egg mix - alternately
with sour cream.

Drop by rounded teaspoonfuls onto a lightly greased cookie sheet.

Bake @ 375° - approximately 7 mins.

Maple Cream Filling

1/2 cup	soft butter or margarine	1	egg yolk
3/4 cup	powdered or icing sugar	1/2 tsp.	vanilla
1/4 tsp.	maple flavoring.		

Cream until well blended - ice cooled cookies.

Gumdrop Cookies

2 cups	flour	1	egg - beaten
1/2 tsp.	salt	3/4 cup	applesauce
2 tsp.	baking powder	1 cup	gumdrops
1/2 tsp.	cinnamon	(cut small/no black ones)	
1/2 cup	shortening	(fruitlets may be used)	
1/2 cup	sugar	1 cup	raisins

Combine together flour - salt - baking powder and cinnamon - set aside.
Cream shortening - add sugar - egg and applesauce - mix well.
Add flour mix - stir till blended - add raisins and gumdrops.

Drop by teaspoon onto a greased cookie sheet - 2 inches apart.
Bake @ 375° - 10 - 15 mins. or lightly browned - transfer to cooling rack.

Makes 4 dozen.

VARIATION: In place of applesauce you may use drained crushed peaches or drained crushed pineapple.

Shortbread

1 lb.	butter	1/2 cup	corn starch
1 cup	powdered/icing sugar	3 1/2-4 cups	flour

Cream butter with mixer - continue to beat as you add 1 cup sugar.
Beat well - add corn starch and about 3 cups of flour.
(More flour may be needed) and beat until light and fluffy.
Roll into balls - place on cookie sheet - flatten with fork dipped in flour.
Bake @ 325° - 12 - 15 minutes - These will appear light in color on top, but browned on the bottom - cool on racks.

Meringues

3	egg whites	1/4 tsp.	cream of tartar
1/8 tsp.	salt	1 tsp.	vinegar
3/4 cup	sugar	1/2 tsp.	vanilla

In mixer bowl place egg whites - cream of tartar - vinegar and salt. Beat till foamy - gradually add sugar in small portions - continually beating until stiff and glossy.

Prepare baking sheet with brown paper or parchment. Place meringue into a pastry bag - pipe mounds or circles with sides built up (spoon may be used).

Place into a 200° oven for 2 hours - leave till completely dry.

OPTION: Heat oven to 350° - TURN OFF OVEN place meringues in oven - leave over night.

MERINGUES MUST BE COMPLETELY DRY

NOTE: If shaped in rounds with sides built up centres may be filled for serving.

* Whipping cream with crushed peppermint candy on top.
* Lemon cream filling with a dollop of cream.

Lemon Squares

Crust

1 cup	flour	1/2 cup	margarine
1	egg	1 tsp.	vanilla

Mix as for pastry - pat into a 9" square pan - bake @ 350° - 10 mins.

Filling   Mix well and cook together until thickened.

1	egg	1/2 cup	sugar
1 tbsp.	butter	Juice and rind from 1 lemon	

Cool and spread over baked base.

Topping

1	egg - beaten	3/4 cup	sugar
2 cups	coconut	1 tsp.	vanilla

Combine and spread over lemon filling - bake @ 325° - approximately 20 - 25 minutes.

Peanut Butter Bars

1 cup	brown sugar	1 1/2 cups	flour
1/2 cup	margarine or butter	1 tsp.	soda
1/2 cup	peanut butter (crunchy/smooth)	1/4 tsp.	salt
		1/2 cup	oatmeal
1 tsp.	vanilla		
1	egg		

Cream together first 5 ingredients - add flour - soda - salt and oatmeal. Press into a 9x9" pan - bake @ 375° - 10 - 12 minutes - cool.

Frosting:

2 tbsp.	butter		
2 tbsp.	peanut butter	2 1/2 tbsp.	milk
1 1/2 cups	powdered/icing sugar		dash of salt

Rice Krispie Caramel Bars

Note: Prepare caramel sauce first - melt together in heavy saucepan and keep on low heat while preparing marshmallows. Both must be ready at the same time.

Caramel Sauce

4	McIntosh Toffee Bars (broken)	1/4 cup	butter
1/2 cup	evaporated milk		

Marshmallow Mix

1/2 cup	margarine	1 tsp.	vanilla
8 cups	miniature marshmallows (or 80 large)	10 cups	Rice Krispies

In micro or large saucepan over med. heat mix and melt together margarine and marshmallows.
Cook together until well blended - stir constantly if using stove top.
Remove from heat - stir in the vanilla.

Place the measured amount of Krispies in a large bowl - pour hot mix over.

Using a spoon, press half the Krispie mix into a lightly greased 9"x13" pan. (Run spoon under hot tap water to prevent sticking.) Spread caramel sauce over this and top with remaining half of Krispies. Chill.

Brownies

1 1/2 cups	brown sugar	1 tsp.	vanilla
1/2 cup	margarine - melted	1 cup	flour
4 tbsp.	cocoa	3/4 cup	chopped nuts
2	eggs		

Combine sugar - cocoa and margarine - add the eggs.
Stir in vanilla - flour and nuts
Spread in a greased 8"x8" pan - bake @ 325° 25 - 30 mins..
DO NOT OVERBAKE. Cool and cover with chocolate icing.

VARIATION: Peppermint Icing
Cream together:

2 oz.	cream cheese	1/8 cup	margarine
2 cups	powdered/icing sugar	1-2 tbsp.	milk
1/2 tsp.	vanilla	1/4 tsp.	peppermint
2-3 drops	green food coloring		extract

Spread over cooled brownies.
Glaze - 1/2 square semi sweet chocolate - melted with 1 tsp.
margarine - drizzle over top.

Cherry Slices

1 cup	butter	2 1/2 cups	flour
1 3/4 cup	sugar	1 1/2 tsp.	baking powder
4	eggs		pinch of salt
1 tsp.	vanilla	1 can	cherry pie filling

Beat together - butter -sugar - eggs and vanilla till light and fluffy.
Gradually add dry ingredients - beat well. Reserve 1 1/2 cups
batter.
Spread remaining batter into a greased 11x17" pan - spread with
pie filling.
Drop reserved batter by spoonfuls over pie filling - spread
carefully. Bake @ 350° for 40 mins.
Sprinkle with powdered sugar or frost with a thin icing - cut into
squares.

Fudgy Brownies

1 cup	butter or margarine	1 cup	flour
4 sqs.	unsweetened chocolate	1 tsp.	salt
2 cups	sugar	1/2 tsp.	baking powder
4	eggs - well beaten	1 cup	chopped nuts
2 tsp.	vanilla		(coarse)

Melt together over low heat or micro - margarine and chocolate.
Stir till completely smooth - remove from heat - add sugar.
Mix in eggs -vanilla and dry ingredients - nuts optional.
Put into a greased metal pan 9x13" - bake @ 325° - approx. 40
minutes. Test for doneness - place tooth pick in centre - should
come out almost clean.
DO NOT OVER BAKE

Icing:

2 sqs.	unsweetened chocolate	1/4 cup	milk
2 tbsp.	margarine	2 cups	powdered /icing sugar

Melt chocolate and margarine together - blend in the milk - add
sugar. Mix well - spread over cooled brownies.

Cherry Bars

1/2 cup	butter	1 cup	chopped walnuts
1 cup	flour	1/2 tsp.	almond flavoring
2 tbsp.	powdered sugar	1/2 cup	maraschino cherries
2	eggs - beaten lightly	1 cup	dates - chopped fine
		1 cup	brown sugar
2 tbsp.	flour	1 cup	coconut
1/2 tsp.	baking powder		

Mix together butter, flour and powdered sugar as for shortbread -
place into a 9" square pan. Bake @ 350° - 15 mins.
Mix remaining ingredients well - spread mixture over baked base -
continue baking till golden brown.
When cooled - cover with orange or lemon icing.

Turtle Bars

1 pkg.	German chocolate cake mix
3/4 cup	melted margarine
1/2 cup	milk or evaporated milk

Mix and stir until dough holds together - press half of dough into a 9x13" pan - bake @ 350° - 6 minutes.

Version #1	**Prepare Version #1 or #2**	Version #2	
4	toffee bars	48-50	caramels (14 oz)
1/2 cup	margarine	1/2 cup	evaporated milk
1 cup	condensed milk	3/4 cup	pecans
3/4 cup	pecans	1 cup	chocolate chips
1 cup	chocolate chips		

In a saucepan over low heat melt toffee and margarine - stir in milk.

Pour over partially baked crust - sprinkle with pecans - then chocolate chips.

Drop spoonfuls of remaining dough over, using a knife to spread. Bake @ 350° - 18 - 20 mins. - cool slightly - refrigerate 30 mins. before cutting.

Date Bars

1 1/2 cups	oatmeal - old fashioned	1 cup	melted butter (must be butter)
1 1/2 cups	flour	1 cup	cut up dates
1 cup	brown sugar	1 cup	water
1/2 tsp.	soda	2 tbsp.	lemon juice
1/4 tsp.	salt	1/4-1/2 cup	sugar -(opt.)

Mix together first six ingredients - pat half of mixture in 9x9" pan.

In a saucepan place - dates and water.
Bring to a boil - cook till thickened - add lemon juice (opt. sugar if desired).
Cook one minute longer - spread evenly over mixture in pan.
Crumble the reserve half of crumbs over the top - lightly press down. Bake @ 350° - 25 mins.
Cut into squares while still warm but not hot - LICK THE KNIFE GENTLY.

VARIATION:
To make this recipe into an apple or rhubarb crisp - grease a 9x9" pan. Put in fruit of choice - sprinkle some sugar over fruit - top with crumb mixture.

A chip on the shoulder is sure indication that there is more wood higher up.

Marzipan Bars

Pie pastry for a 9" square pan.

1/2 cup	margarine	2	eggs
2/3 cup	sugar	2/3 cup	flour
		1/2 tsp.	almond flavoring
	raspberry jam		
	red and green food coloring		

Line bottom of pan with pastry - 1/4" thick.
Cover pastry with thin layer of jam - your choice.
Cream margarine and sugar - add eggs - beat until light - stir in flour and flavoring.

Divide batter in half - color one portion light pink - other green.
Gently spoon and spread green batter over jam layer.
Spread pink layer over this.

Bake @ 375° for 30 - 35 mins. - frost with almond flavored white icing. Cut into bars.

Almond Bar

Base:

1 1/4 cup	flour	1/3 cup	butter
3 tbsp.	powdered/icing sugar	2/3 cup	brown sugar
1/3 cup	butter	1/3 cup	cream
		1 tsp.	vanilla
		1 cup	almonds (slivered)

Combine flour - powdered sugar and butter - press into 9x9" pan.
Bake @ 350° for 10 mins..

In a heavy saucepan melt butter - add sugar and cream.
Boil for 3 mins. - remove from heat - stir in vanilla and almonds.
Spread evenly over the base crust - bake 20 mins. - cool - cut into squares.

Choco Cherry Bars

1 1/4 cup	flour	1/2 tsp.	salt
2/3 cup	brown sugar - divided	1	egg
3/4 cup	margarine - softened	1 1/2 cups	chocolate chips
1 1/2 cups	salted mixed nuts (chopped - coarsely)		
1 1/2 cup	red and green cherries - halves		

Combine flour with 1/3 cup brown sugar and margarine.
Mix to resemble coarse crumbs - press onto an ungreased cookie sheet 10x14".
Bake @ 350° for 12 mins.

Meanwhile beat the egg slightly in a bowl - stir in remaining sugar and salt.
Add the nuts - cherries and chips - toss lightly to coat.
Spoon mixture over the baked layer - press firmly with a spoon to adhere layers.

Bake @ 350° for 20 mins. - cool - cut into bars.

Rocky Road Bars

Base: Line a 9x13" pan with whole graham wafers.

Topping:

1 cup	butterscotch chips
3/4 cup	butter or margarine
1	egg
1/2 cup	powdered/icing sugar
4 cups	miniature marshmallows
	fine coconut

Over low heat combine chips - butter - egg and sugar.
When melted - remove from heat - add marshmallows.
Spread butterscotch mixture over wafer base - sprinkle with coconut - cool before cutting.

Chip Caramel Bars

| 3 | toffee bars | 2/3 cup | evaporated milk |
| 2 tbsp. | margarine | | |

Combine the above ingredients in a saucepan and melt over low heat till smooth - set aside.

2 cups	flour	1 tsp.	soda
1 3/4 cup	oatmeal - large flake	1/2 tsp.	salt
1 cup	brown sugar	1 cup	margarine (melted)

Combine the above dry ingredients - add margarine - mix till crumbly.
Reserve 2 cups of mixture - press remainder into a greased 9x13" pan.
Bake @ 350° - 12 mins. or lightly browned - remove from oven.
Pour toffee mixture over base in the pan.

Combine the following - sprinkle evenly over toffee mix:

1 cup white chocolate chips
1 cup slivered almonds
2 SKOR bars - crushed

Spread reserve crumbs on top. Press down lightly with fork.

Return to oven - bake 20 - 22 mins. or till golden - cool before cutting.

NOTE: This square is naughty rich *but nice*.

Do not store crisp and soft cookies together in the same container.

Never Fail Pie Pastry

1 lb.	lard (room temp.)	1 tsp.	sugar
5 cups	flour	1	egg
1 tsp.	salt	1 tbsp.	vinegar
1 tsp.	baking powder		

Combine lard - flour - salt - sugar and baking powder - make a coarse crumble mix.
In a measuring cup place egg and vinegar - mix with a fork.
Fill cup measure with cold water - add to the flour mix.
Combine - using hands to make a soft dough.

Divide dough into 5 or 6 balls - wrap individually in waxed paper.
Place into a plastic bag - refrigerate a couple of days or freeze.

When needed take out of freezer in advance - thaw - roll out on floured surface.
Turn several times as you roll - approx. 1/4" thick - gently place on pie pan.
Prick sides and bottom with a fork about 12 times - chill.
Use dough for desired recipes - tarts or pies.
If using for a double crust pie - make slits in the top for steam vents.

Refrigerator Pie Pastry

5 1/2 cups	flour	2 tsp.	salt
1 tsp.	baking powder	2 1/3 cups	shortening

Mix the above into a crumb mixture - place into a ziplock bag - store in the refrigerator.

To make one single crust:
Use: 1 1/4 cup dry mix   2-4 tbsp. cold water

Mix and combine only till dough sticks together - roll out on a floured surface.

Baked Pastry Shell

On a generously floured surface place approx. 1 cup pastry - pat down with finger tips to form approx. 5" circle. Turn over always making sure the surface underneath is always floured. Sprinkle a little more flour on top and begin rolling from centre out until 2" larger than pie plate. You will need to turn pastry several more times to achieve this. Fold gently in half and transfer to pie plate. Place loosely in pan - not stretching but easing in gently. Trim overhang edge to 1" if needed and fold under at edge - using thumbs press together at 1" intervals to flute and stick pastry to top edge of pie plate.

Prick bottom and sides thoroughly with fork.

Bake @ 425° - 8 - 10 mins. or until lightly browned.

To avoid shrinkage refrigerate dough for 20 - 30 mins. before baking.

NOTE: If using pyrex be sure to place a piece of foil under plate or it may break because of placing on a hot rack.

Butter Tarts

2	eggs - well beaten	1 tsp.	vanilla
1 cup	brown sugar	1 tsp.	vinegar
2 tbsp.	light cream		raisins
2 tbsp.	melted butter		

Into a pastry lined tart pan place approx. 7 raisins or more into each shell.

Mix together - eggs - sugar - butter - cream - vanilla and vinegar. Fill shells 3/4 full with filling.

Bake @ 350° - 20 mins. or until light brown.

VARIATION: Pecans may be used in place of raisins.

88

Elyce's Cream Pie Filling

2/3 cup	sugar	2 3/4 cups	milk
1/2 tsp.	salt	3	eggs - separated
3 tbsp.	corn starch	1 tbsp.	butter
1 tbsp.	flour	1 1/2 tsp.	vanilla

Mix together - sugar - salt - corn starch and flour - graduallyadd 2 3/4 cups of cold milk.
Cook over moderate heat, stirring constantlyuntil it thickens and boils.
Boil 1 minute - remove from heat.

Beat 3 egg yolks, slightly - slowly add some of the pudding mixture to the egg yolks - about a cup measurement.

Add the egg mixture to the rest of the pudding and cook 1 minute more.

Blend in 1 tbsp. butter and 1 1/2 tsp. vanilla.

VARIATION:

Coconut Cream Pie
Add 1 cup of coconut when you add the butter and vanilla.

Banana Cream Pie
Line your baked pie crust with bananas and then top with the cream filling.

Chocolate Cream Pie
Add 3 - 4 tbsp. cocoa with sugar mixture. To make this extra delicious - sprinkle hot baked pie shell with chocolate chips. Fill pie with chocolate cream - while still warm sprinkle more chocolate chips on top. Cool - serve with whipped cream.

NOTE: To make a rich cream pie - use 2 cups of milk and 3/4 cup of half and half. (Can't do this if you are watching your waistline!)

Flapper Pie

Crust:

1 1/2 cups	graham wafer crumbs
1/4 cup	sugar
1/4 tsp.	cinnamon
1/2 cup	margarine - melted

Combine and mix well - reserve 1/4 cup for topping.
Press remainder into a 9" pie plate.
Bake @ 350° - 10 mins.

Prepare Elyce's Cream Pie Filling
Pour filling into pie crust - top with the meringue (see below).

Meringue:

3	egg whites (room temperature)
1/4 tsp.	cream of tartar
6 tbsp.	sugar

Beat egg whites and cream of tartar till frothy, gradually add the
sugar while beating.
Beat 5 - 7 mins. or till very stiff.

Spread meringue over filling to the edge of the pie, sprinkle
reserve crumbs over the top.
Bake @ 350° for 20 mins.

NOTE: Butter your knife before cutting a meringue pie. You will
get a clean cut without damaging the meringue.

Glazed Strawberry Pie

1 cup + 2 tbsp.	sugar	3 tbsp.	water
1 cup	water	3 tsp.	red food coloring
1/8 tsp.	salt	2 tbsp. + 2 tsp.	strawberry jello
3 tbsp.	corn starch	1 qt.	ripe strawberries

Combine sugar - 1 cup water and salt.
Bring to a boil - add corn starch that has been mixed with the 3 tbsp. of water.

Boil until clear - remove from heat.
Stir in food coloring and jello - cool to lukewarm.
Place washed - drained - cooled strawberries in a baked pie shell and pour glaze over the stawberries.
Refrigerate - serve with whipped cream.

NOTE: Make this 8 hrs. before serving to allow time to set.

THIS IS THE BEST ! ! !

Cherry Pie

On a floured board roll out pie pastry for 9" pie plate.

1 - 19 oz. can	cherry pie filling
1 tsp.	almond flavoring
1/4 cup	white sugar
1 tbsp.	corn starch

In a bowl combine sugar and corn starch.
Stir into cherries - add flavoring. Place filling in pie shell.

Roll out another piece of pastry for pie top.
Cut into 3/4" strips - place over filled pie to make to make a lattice design in a flat or twisted style.
Moisten ends to seal - trim overlapping edges - flute edge.

Bake @ 350° - 35 - 40 mins. - nicely browned.

Pumpkin Pie

1 - 9"	unbaked pie crust		

Filling:

1 1/2 cups	canned pumpkin	2 tbsp.	flour
1/2 cup	brown sugar	1 tsp.	cinnamon
1/2 cup	white sugar	1 tsp.	ginger
1/2 tsp.	cloves	1/2 tsp.	salt
2	eggs - slightly beaten		
2 tbsp.	concentrated orange juice (opt.)		
1 cup	canned milk or light cream		

Combine pumpkin - sugars - salt - flour and spices.
Add eggs - orange juice and canned milk.
Pour into unbaked pie crust.

Bake @ 400° - 15 mins. - reduce heat to 325° - 45 mins. or till a knife blade comes out clean when inserted in centre.
If crust gets to dark - cover with a foil ring.

Blueberry Pie

Pie pastry for a double 9" pie crust.

4-5 cups	fresh or frozen blueberries		
3/4 cup	sugar	3/4 cup	water - divided
1 tsp.	lemon juice	4 tbsp.	corn starch

Place blueberries in a saucepan together with 1/2 cup water - sugar and lemon juice.
Mix together corn starch and remaining water.
Bring blueberries to a boil - remove from heat and stir in the corn starch mixture.

Place filling into a prepared unbaked pie crust.
Moisten edges with water and place top crust over.
Press down and crimp edges - perforate top - sprinkle with sugar.
Bake @ 375° - 30 - 35 mins. or till crust is browned.

Lemon Pie

3	egg yolks	1 3/4	water
1/4 cup	water	4-5 tbsp.	lemon juice
1 1/4 cup	sugar	1 tsp.	grated lemon rind
6 tbsp.	corn starch	1 tbsp.	butter

Mix slightly beaten egg yolks with 1/4 cup of water and set aside.

Combine sugar - corn starch and 1 3/4 cup water.
Bring to a boil and cook until thick and clear.

Add egg yolk mixture and cook 1 min. longer.

Remove from heat.
Add juice - rind and butter.

NOTE: This can be done in the microwave oven, never scorches.
Makes a great pudding as well.

Top with meringue (page 90) or whipped cream.

Apple Pie

Pie pastry for a double 9" pie crust.

5-6 med.	tart aples - peeled and sliced		
3/4 cup	sugar	1 tsp.	cinnamon
1/4 tsp.	nutmeg	1 tbsp.	butter
2 tbsp.	flour		

Combine apples - sugar - spices and flour.
Place into unbaked pastry lined pie pan - dot with butter.
Moisten edges with water - place a rolled pastry top over the filling
- crimp and seal edges.
Make slits for steam vents in top - sprinkle with sugar and
cinnamon.
Bake @ 400° for 15 mins. - lower heat to 350°.
Bake 30 mins. longer or until crust is golden brown.

Pecan Pie

2/3 cup	brown sugar	2/3 cup	white corn syrup
3 tbsp.	butter	2	eggs - beaten
	dash of salt	1/2 tsp.	vanilla
1 cup	pecans		

Cover your unbaked pie crust with pecans. Combine rest of ingredients and pour over pecans.
Bake 15 mins. @ 375° and then bake for 20 mins. @ 350°.

Putting a foil ring on the edge of the crust will keep it from getting too brown.

If you put the pecans in the bottom of the pan they will come to the top but the syrup mixture glazes the nuts and your nuts won't burn.

Raisin Pie

Pastry for double crust pie.

2 cups	boiling water	2 tbsp.	flour
2 1/4 cups	raisins	1/2 tsp.	salt
2 tsp.	grated lemon rind	1	egg - beaten
1 cup	brown sugar		pinch of nutmeg (optional)

Comine boiling water - raisins and lemon rind in saucepan.
Simmer 10 mins. - combine sugar - flour and salt.
Gradually add dry mix to hot mixture - stirring constantly.
Cook until thick - remove from heat.

Add a small amount of the cooked mixture to beaten egg - then add this to the remaining mixture in saucepan.
Return to heat - cook one minute - remove from heat - cool.

Line pie plate with rolled out pastry - fill with cooled mixture.
Put on pastry top - cut a 4" X in the centre of top crust - fold back tips. Trim and flute edges. Bake @ 425° - 35 - 40 mins. or till golden brown.

Sour Cream Raisin Pie

1 single baked pie crust.

2	eggs - separated	1/2 tsp.	cinnamon
1 cup	raisins	1/8 tsp.	salt
1 cup	sour cream	1 tsp.	baking soda
1/2 cup	sugar	2 tbsp.	sugar

Separate the eggs - set whites aside.
Into a saucepan put 2 egg yolks - raisins - sour cream - 1/2 cup sugar - cinnamon and salt.
Bring to a boil - reduce heat to med. - cook and stir until a thick pudding (approx. 5 mins.).
Remove from heat - stir in baking soda.
Cover with plastic wrap - cool in fridge till chilled.

Prepare meringue - beating 2 egg whites till foamy - gradually add 2 tbsp. sugar - continue to beat till stiff peaks form.
Spoon filling into baked pie shell - spread evenly - top with meringue.
Be sure to spread meringue to outer edge - covering the filling well.

Bake @ 400° for 10 mins. - or till top is browned. - Cool.

Coconut Jam Tarts

Prepared pie pastry.

2	eggs - well beaten	1 tbsp.	butter
1 cup	sugar	1 cup	coconut
1 tsp.	vanilla		raspberry jam

Line tart tin with pastry.
Combine all ingredients except jam.
Into each tart shell put a teaspoon of raspberry jam.
Top with the above mixture.
Bake @ 350° - approx. 20 mins.

Baking Powder Biscuits

1/2 cup	lard or shortening	2 cups	flour
1/2 tsp.	salt	1 tbsp.	sugar (opt.)
4 tsp.	baking powder	3/4 cup	milk

Combine - flour - sugar - salt and baking powder.
Cut in the lard - using a fork make a coarse crumb mix.
Make a well in centre - add liquid all at once.
Stir just till dough clings together.

Turn out on a lightly floured board - pat into 3/4" thickness.
Using a sharp edged 2 1/2" round cutter press out rounds - place
on a baking sheet.   Makes 10 - 12
Bake @425° - 10 - 12 mins.

NOTE: Biscuits will have soft sides if placed close together on
baking sheet. Margarine may be substituted in place of lard or
shortening.

Buttermilk makes these even better - increase liquid to 1 cup.

Corn Bread

1 cup	yellow cornmeal	1/2 tsp.	salt
1/2 cup	all-purpose flour	1/8 tsp.	baking soda
2 1/2 tsp.	baking powder	2	eggs
1 tsp.	sugar	1 cup	buttermilk
		2 tbsp.	cooking oil

Stir together the cornmeal - flour - baking powder - sugar - salt
and baking soda. Make a well in the center - set aside.

Mix together the eggs - buttermilk and cooking oil.
Add the egg mixture to the dry ingredients all at once.
Stir till smooth.

Pour into greased 9" square pan - bake at 350° for 25 mins.
Delicious served warm for breakfast with butter and corn syrup.

Oatmeal Muffins

1 cup	oatmeal	1 1/2 cups	flour
1 cup	sour milk	1 tsp.	baking powder
1	egg - slightly beaten	1 /2 tsp.	soda
1/2 cup	oil	3/4 tsp.	salt
3/4 cup	brown sugar		

Mix together oatmeal - milk - egg - oil and sugar.
Let stand at least 15 mins. - combine the rest of ingredients.
Stir together only till blended - put into greased muffin tins.

Bake @ 350° - 20 - 25 mins.   Yield = 12 muffins.

VARIATION: To the above recipe you may add your choice of fruits. These must be added together with the dry ingredients.

Suggest: Blueberries - Cranberries - Shredded Cheese - Nuts etc.

Bran Muffins

1 1/2 cup	bran	1 cup	flour
1 cup	buttermilk	1/2 tsp.	salt
3/4 cup	brown sugar	1 tsp.	baking powder
3 tbsp.	molasses	1 tsp.	soda
1	egg	1/2 cup	raisins (opt.)
1/2 cup	oil	1/2 cup	chopped dates (opt.)

Mix bran - milk - sugar - molasses - oil and egg - let rest 15 mins.
Add remainder of ingredients - stir only till blended.

Put into greased muffin tins.

Bake @ 350° - 20 mins.   Yield = 12 muffins.

Sunrise Muffins

2 cups	flour	2 cups	carrots	
1 cup	sugar		(finely shredded)	
1/2 tsp.	baking powder	1 cup	apples	
2 tsp.	cinnamon		(finely chopped)	
2 tsp.	baking soda	1/2 cup	raisins	
1/2 tsp.	salt	1/2 cup	chopped nuts	
3	eggs	1/2 cup	shredded coconut	
3/4 cup	oil	1/4 cup	sunflower seeds	
2 tsp.	vanilla			

Combine dry ingredients - stir in carrots - fruits - coconut - nuts and seeds. In a separate bowl mix eggs - oil and vanilla - add to flour mix. Stir just till moistened.
Lightly grease 18 - 2 1/4" muffin cups or line with paper baking cups.
Fill with batter until almost full.

Bake @ 350° - 25 mins. or till top springs back when lightly touched. Set on rack to cool for 5 mins..
Remove from pan. Nice served warm.

NOTE: Bran muffins served with a slice of cheddar cheese and a cup of tea make a delightful snack.

Coconut Cherry Loaf

1 cup	butter	1/4 tsp.	salt
1 cup	sugar	2 cups	flour (divided)
5	eggs	1 cup	shredded coconut
1 tsp.	baking powder	1/2 lb.	glazed cherries
1/2 tsp.	mace		(whole)

Makes large loaf.

Sift together 1 cup of flour - mace - salt and baking powder - set aside.

Mix reserve flour (1 cup) with cherries and coconut - set aside.

In mixer bowl - cream together butter and sugar.
Add eggs one at a time - beating well after each addition.
Blend in the flour mix - fold in floured fruit mixture - combine well.

Line a loaf pan - 9x5x3" with foil - grease well.
Spoon in the batter - bake @ 300° for 1 1/2 - 1 3/4 hours.

NOTE: This loaf should ripen a few days before slicing allowing the flavors to blend.
Top with a cherry flavored icing - may serve as a Christmas loaf.

Banana Loaf

1 cup	sugar	1 1/2 cups	flour
1/2 cup	shortening	1/2 tsp.	salt
1 cup	mashed bananas (3)	1 tsp.	soda
2	eggs - well beaten		

Blend dry ingredients together with shortening till crumbly.
Add eggs and bananas. Fold together quickly - DO NOT OVERMIX. Pour into greased loaf pan - bake @ 350° - 40 - 45 mins. Let stand 5 mins. - turn out on rack to cool.
NOTE: OVER-RIPE BANANAS may be frozen whole with peels on.

Pumpkin Bread

1 1/2 cups	sugar	1 3/4 cups	flour
1/2 cup	oil	1 tsp.	soda
2	eggs	1/2 tsp.	baking powder
1 cup	pumpkin - canned	1/2 tsp.	salt
1/2 tsp.	cloves	1/2 tsp.	nutmeg
1/2 tsp.	cinnamon	1/4 cup	water
1/2 cup	raisins	1/2 cup	chopped nuts
1/2 cup	candied cherries		

Mix together - sugar - oil - eggs - pumpkin and water.

Add dry ingredients together with raisins - nuts and cherries.
Stir to combine - put into a greased loaf pan.

Bake @ 350° 45 - 50 mins.

Graham Nut Bread

2 1/3 cups	graham wafer crumbs	3	eggs - separated
2 tsp.	baking powder	1/2 cup	butter
1 tsp.	grated lemon rind	1 cup	sugar
3/4 cups	chopped walnuts	3/4 cup	milk

Combine wafer crumbs - baking powder - lemon rind and walnuts.
Cream butter - gradually beat in sugar - add egg yolks one at a
time - beating well after each addition.

Add dry ingredients to the creamed mixture - alternately with milk.
Mix lightly after each addition.
Beat egg whites till stiff - fold into above mix.

Pour into a greased loaf pan. Bake @ 350° for 1 hour & 10 mins..
Cool on rack 10 mins. - remove from pan - cool completely.

Date Loaf

2 cups	chopped dates	1 tsp.	vanilla
1 tsp.	baking soda	1 1/2 cups	flour
1 cup	boiling water	1 1/2 tsp.	baking powder
1 cup	brown sugar	1/4 tsp.	salt
1 1/2 tbsp.	melted butter	1 cup	chopped nuts
1	egg	1 cup	raisins (opt.)

In a bowl combine together dates and baking soda.
Pour boiling water over dates - mix well - set aside.

Combine sugar - butter - egg and vanilla - blend with dates.
Mix flour - baking powder and salt - stir into above mixture.
Add nuts and raisins - pour batter in a well greased loaf pan -
9x5x3"

Bake @ 350° for 1 hour.

Lemon Loaf

6 tbsp.	shortening	1 1/2 cups	flour
1 cup	sugar	1 tsp.	baking powder
2	eggs	1/8 tsp.	salt
1/2 cup	milk		zest of 1 lemon

Cream together - shortening - sugar - eggs.
Combine - flour - baking powder and salt.
Add to creamed mixture alternately with milk.
Stir in the lemon zest.

Spoon batter into a well greased loaf pan - 9x5x3".
Bake @ 350° for one hour.

Remove from oven - spoon topping mix over while still warm.

Topping: Combine together 1/2 cup sugar and 2 tbsp. lemon
juice.
Delicious served warm.

Basic Bread or Buns

1 cup	luke warm water	1 tsp.	sugar
2 pkg.	yeast		

Combine in a bowl - set aside - let stand 10 mins.

3 cups	warm water	1 1/2 tbsp.	salt
2 tbsp.	sugar	1/3 cup	melted lard
8 1/2-9 cups flour			or shortening

In large mixer bowl combine yeast mixture - water - salt - sugar and lard.
Add 4 cups of flour - mix on medium speed for 5 mins.

In large mixing bowl put in 4 cups flour - add yeast sponge mix. Mix with wooden spoon - knead in remaining flour to make a soft dough - (if used for bread, dough should be a little more firm).

Cover - let rise in warm place till double in bulk - knead - let rest 10 mins.

Shape into buns or loaves - place into greased pans.
Let rise till double in size.

Bake @ 350° - loaves 35 - 40 mins. - buns 20 - 25 mins.
Yields = 4 loaves or 3 dozen buns.

NOTE: When shaping dough balls to make buns - grease hands lightly to prevent sticking.

Whole Wheat Bread

2 pkg.	yeast	1/2 cup	sugar
1 1/2 tsp.	sugar	1/4 cup	lard or shortening
1/2 cup	warm water	3 cups	warm water
1 tbsp.	salt	2 cups	whole wheat flour
8-9 cups	white flour - divided		

In a bowl combine yeast - 1 1/2 tsp. sugar - 1/2 cup warm water - set aside.

In a large bowl - combine salt - sugar - lard - 3 cups water. Stir in whole wheat flour and 2 cups of the white flour - add yeast mix - beat with a beater for 3 mins. - add 6 cups more flour.

Knead dough with hands to make a moderately stiff dough - smooth and elastic.

Turn out on a floured board - add extra flour if needed - knead for 5 mins.
Place in a greased bowl - cover - let rise till double size - punch down - repeat rising.

Shape into 4 loaves - place into greased loaf pans - cover with a damp cloth.
Let rise till double size.

Bake @ 350° - 30 - 35 mins. - brush top with margarine (opt.).

NOTE: To test a bread loaf for doneness, tap the crust - it will have a hollow sound.

Remove bread from pans immediately - cool on wire rack.

For a soft crust - cover bread lightly with a towel.

French Bread

2 pkgs.	yeast	2 tsp.	salt
1/2 tsp.	sugar	1/4 cup	sugar
1/2 cup	warm water	1/3 cup	Crisco
2 cups	boiling water	6 cups	flour - divided

Mix together - yeast - warm water and 1/2 tsp. sugar - set aside - 10 mins.

In a mixing bowl combine boiling water - salt - sugar and Crisco - cool to luke warm - add the yeast mixture - stir well.

Add 3 cups of flour to yeast mix - mix well - let stand 5 mins. Add in remainder 3 cups flour - combine and knead together. Grease top - cover - let rest 10 mins. - punch down - repeat this 5 times.

Divide into 2 equal portions - roll out as for cinnamon rolls - roll into a loaf.
Place on a greased baking sheet - cut 3 slashes diagonallyinto top - 1/4 - 1/2" deep.

Let rise 1 hour - bake @ 400° - 20 mins. - EXCELLENT!

Elly's Yeast Buns

(Excellent for Doughnuts)

2 tbsp.	instant yeast	1/2 cup	cooking oil
1/4 cup	sugar	2	eggs
4 cups	warm water	4 cups	flour
4 tsp.	salt	6 1/2-7 cups	flour

Using a mixer on low speed - beat together for 2 mins. the yeast - sugar and water.
Add the salt - eggs - oil and the 4 cups of flour - beat till bubbles form.

Place mixture into a large bowl - add 6 cups of flour - work with hands.
Knead till you have a smooth dough and not sticky (may need the extra flour).
Dough should pull away from sides of bowl and hands.

Cover and let rise in a warm place for 45 mins. - knead down.
Let rise another 30 mins. - knead down - let rise 30 mins. more.

Pull off small portions of dough - shape and roll into bun form - with greased finger tips.
Place into 3 well greased 9x13" pans (15 in each pan) makes approx. 45 buns.

Bake @ 350° - 20 mins.
Remove from pans to a cooling rack - lightly cover with tea towel (keeps tops from becoming crusty).

Cinnamon Buns

Caramel Rolls

4 cups	warm water	1 cup	milk powder
3/4 cup	sugar	2 tbsp.	instant yeast
1 tbsp.	salt	3/4 cup	margarine
3	eggs - beaten	10-11 cups	flour - divided

Cream margarine - add sugar - salt - eggs and water. Combine 4 cups of the flour - milk powder and yeast - add to the above - beat with mixer 5 mins.

In a large mixing bowl place 5 cups of flour - add the batter.
Stir with wooden spoon until blended - knead using hands - until it forms a soft dough - adding extra flour as needed. Dough should pull away from sides of bowl.

Cover with plastic - set in a warm place - let rise for 1 hour.
Knead down - let rise 30 mins. - divide dough into 2 equal portions.

Roll out dough on a lightly floured surface - into a rectangle - 16x20".
Spread with a thin layer of softened margarine to within 1/2" of edges.
Sprinkle half of sugar mixture (below) over margarine.

Starting at long side - roll up in jelly roll fashion. Pinch edge to seal.
With a sharp knife cut into 1 1/2 - 2" peices.
Generously grease 3 pans - 9x13" - place rolls on pan - let rise 30 - 40 mins. Bake @ 375° approx. 25 mins.

VARIATION: For sticky buns use the caramel sauce as given.
Spoon caramel sauce (pecans opt.) into pans before placing rolls on top reserving a little to drizzle over unbaked rolls before putting into the oven. When removing from oven turn out on cooling racks placed over waxed paper.

Caramel Sauce

1/2 cup	brown sugar
1/2 cup	white syrup**
1/2 cup	margarine
1/2 cup	cream or ice cream
	pecans - optional

Sugar Mixture

1 1/2 cups	brown sugar
3/4 cup	white sugar
6 tsp.	cinnamon
	MIX TOGETHER

**White sugar may be substituted for white syrup.
Combine in saucepan.
Bring to a boil - boil 1 min.
Remove from heat.

Monkey Bread

Use Cinnamon Dough Recipe or Elly's Yeast Bun Dough

Grease tube pan - pinch off dough pieces - approx. size of a walnut.
Roll balls in a combined mix of cinnamon and sugar.
Gently lay in pan - make 3 layers.

Pour caramel sauce over. See Cinnamon Buns.
Cover wire rack with foil - turn out buns while still warm.
Bake @ 350° - 30 - 35 mins.

Sweet Roll Dough
Mashed Potatoes Sweet Roll Dough

1/2 cup	water - luke warm	3/4 cup	soft margarine or shortening
1 tsp.	sugar		
2 pkgs.	yeast	1/2 cup	mashed potatoes
3	eggs - well beaten	2 tsp.	salt
2/3 cup	sugar	3 cups	warm milk/water
8 1/2 - 9 cups flour divided			

Mix together - yeast - water and 1 tsp. sugar - set aside - 10 mins..
Beat together well - eggs - sugar - margarine - potatoes and salt.
Add in yeast mix - beat well once again.
Slowly add milk and 3 cups flour - mix well - add in 5 1/2 cups of flour.
Knead till dough has elasticity to make a soft dough.
Add more flour if needed - when dough begins to leave sides of bowl turn out on a floured surface - using hands - knead - knead - knead.
If using a bread mixer - mix 5 mins. - place dough in a greased bowl.
Cover with a damp cloth - let rise in a warm draft free spot for 1 1/2 - 2 hours.
USE DOUGH for the desired recipe you wish to make.
See Sweet Dough Variations: Cinnamon Buns or Kuchen.

Sweet Dough Variations

Bienenstich   Into a 9" round greased pan press enough dough to make a 3/4" thick bottom crust - prick with a fork.
Combine and cook together all ingredients except whipping cream - cook for 3 mins.

1/2 cup	sliced almonds	2 tbsp.	light cream
1/4 cup	brown sugar	1 tbsp.	honey or syrup
1 tbsp.	margarine	1 tsp.	vanilla
	whipped cream - sweetened		

Cool slightly - spread over dough - let rise till double in size.
Bake @ 350° for 20 mins.
To serve - slice in two layers - spread with whipped cream - replace top layer - cut in wedges to serve.

Fruit Ring Use Cinnamon Bun dough method. Add into the cinnamon sugar mix - nuts - raisins - and cherries. Roll up - but do not slice - place on a greased baking sheet in a ring form. Seal ends of ring together by moistening the ends of roll with water - pinch together. Slash top at 5" intervals 1/2" deep.
Bake @ 350° - 30 - 35 mins.
Before serving - decorate with icing - cherries and nuts.

Tea Ring   Prepare as for Cinnamon Buns in a roll - cut into 3/4" slices. Grease a 9" round pan - place in slices so each one overlaps slightly to form a circle.
Spread with 1/2 cup streusel crumbs (below) let rise till double in size.
Bake @ 350° - 20 - 25 mins.
To serve decorate with icing - sprinkle with nuts (opt.).

Streusel Crumbs   Mix together till crumbly:

1 cup	flour
1/2 cup	sugar
1/2 cup	butter

Bake Day Surprises

1 cup	**sour cream**	**1 cup**	**brown sugar**
1 tsp.	**soda**	**1 tsp.**	**cinnamon**

Mix together the ingredients for the sauce - set aside.

Take plain bread dough or sweet dough - make into balls about the size of a bun (1 1/2" - 2").

Place buns into a deep greased baking pan - let dough rise - approx. 30 - 40 mins.
When buns are ready to bake pour the sauce over top.

Bake @ 350° - 15 - 20 mins. or till brown and look baked.

* Granny Itterman used to make these all the time.

Elephant Ears

Use Elly's Yeast Bun Dough

As per recipe - after the last rise of dough - DO NOT KNEAD DOWN.

With a sharp knife - cut off pieces of dough (small egg size).
Stretch out pieces to approx. 1/2" thickness.

Fry in hot oil - drain on paper towel.

These are great served as a snack on bake day.
Corn syrup goes well or shake in a bag with sugar or icing sugar.

Fruit Kuchen and Gusse
Use Sweet Dough Recipe or Cinnamon Bun Recipe

Spread dough 1/2 - 3/4" thick into a lightly greased 9" round pan. Prick dough with a fork - place desired fruit on top - ie: apple slices - apricot or plum halves - cut side up - or rhubarb cut in 1/2" pieces etc. Sprinkle with sugar as needed - pour gusse over (see below).

Gusse may be divided - half put on before fruit is placed - remainder over fruit.

Kuchen may be topped with streusel crumbs before baking. Gusse may be drizzled over to keep crumbs in place. Let rise 10 - 15 mins. - bake @ 350° - 25 - 30 mins.

Gusse Custard
2	eggs - beaten
1 cup	sweet/sour cream
1/2 cup	sugar
1/2 tsp.	vanilla flavoring
2 tbsp.	flour

Mix well (enough for 2-3 Kuchen)

Streusel Crumbs
3/4 cup	sugar
1 cup	flour
1/2 cup	butter
1 tsp.	almond flavoring
	dash of salt

Mix together to make coarse crumbs.

VARIATION:
Cottage Cheese Kuchen
1 lb.	cottage cheese - dry curd
1 cup	sugar
3	egg whites

With mixer beat cottage cheese - sugar and egg whites till smooth.
Spoon over dough - should be 1/2 - 3/4" thick - sprinkle generously with cinnamon - bake @ 350° till crust is brown and cheese is firm.

Cream Cheese Kuchen
Prepare - follow instructions as for Cottage Cheese Kuchen.
Beat together till smooth:

1-8 oz. pkg.	cream cheese
1	egg - beaten
3/4 cup	sugar
2 tsp.	vanilla
1/8 tsp.	salt

110

Doughnuts

Use Elly's Yeast Bun Dough or Cinnamon Bun Dough

Roll out dough on a lightly floured surface to approx. 1" thickness - cut with a floured doughnut cutter.
Place on a floured tea towel spacing well for rising. Cover with plastic - let rise approx. one hour - scraps maybe re-rolled.
In a heavy pot or deep fry pan - heat depth of 3" of oil.

Watch carefully - do not leave unattended.

When oil is hot - transfer doughnuts and place into oil (avoid splashing).
Place top side of doughnut into oil first.
Cook till light brown - then turn - oil should be hot enough so they cook fairly quick and yet well cooked (not doughy in the centre).
Sample one to test doneness.

Drain on cooling rack which has been placed on a cookie sheet.
When slightly cooled transfer to a cake pan which is lined with paper towel.
Set doughnuts on edge - to cool completely.

To serve - warm slightly - shake in a bag with powdered/icing or granulated sugar.
Doughnuts can also be glazed or iced with vanilla - chocolate - maple or caramel icing.

May be frozen in plastic bags if desired.

Doughnut Glaze
Mix together:

| 1 cup | powdered/icing sugar | 1 tsp. | butter |
| 1/2 cup | water (warm) | 1 tsp. | vanilla |

Enae's Twisters - Umges

1/4 cup	warm water
1 tsp.	sugar
1 pkg.	yeast

Combine - set aside - let rest 10 mins.

3	eggs - beaten	3/4 cup	milk
3/4 cup	sugar	3/4 cup	whipping cream
5 cups	flour - divided	1 tsp.	vanilla
4 tsp.	baking powder	1 1/4 tsp.	salt

(Heat milk and cream until warm.)

Beat eggs and sugar till slightly thickened.
Add milk - cream - vanilla - yeast mixture and 2 cups of flour.
Beat in mixer bowl for 3 - 4 mins.

Mix together and add remainder of flour - baking powder and salt.
Knead to make a soft dough.
You may need to add an extra 1/2 cup of flour.

Roll out on a floured board to a rectangle 15"x20".
Cut into 3" squares - cover and let rest 20 mins.
Make a slit with a knife in centre of each square and pull one
corner through slit.

Deep fry in hot oil - turn as needed to brown each side.
Place on paper towel to drain.
Serve with a sprinkle of powdered sugar.

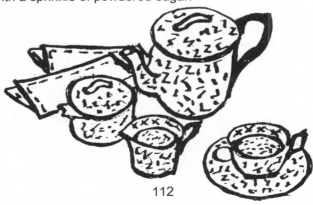

Scuffles

1/4 cup	warm water	1 tsp.	sugar
1 pkg.	yeast		

Combine ingredients - set aside - let stand 10 mins.

3 cups	flour	2	eggs - beaten
3 tbsp.	sugar	1/2 cup	milk
1/2 tsp.	salt		
1 cup	butter or margarine		

Mix flour - sugar - salt and butter - to a coarse crumblymix.
Add eggs - milk and yeast mix - stir together.
Knead until dough is soft (add a little more milk if too stiff).
Place in a greased bowl - cover - place in refrigerator overnight.

Cinnamon/Sugar Mix: 1 cup sugar - 2 tsp. cinnamon

Next day divide dough into four pieces.
Roll each portion in a round as for pie crust - 1/4" thick.
Sprinkle both sides with cinnamon/sugar mix as you roll it out.
When rolled out sprinkle with more cinnamon sugar mix.
Cut round into 8 wedges - roll up startng at wide edge.
Place on ungreased cookie sheet - let rise 45 mins.
Bake @ 350° - 15 mins.

Hot Cross Buns

Use Cinnamon Bun Dough Recipe - Prepare 1/2 recipe size.

Into last addition of flour add:

2 tbsp.	cinnamon	1/2 cup	glazed mixed fruit
1/2 cup	raisins		

When dough ready for pans - shape into dinner buns - place on greased pan.
Cut cross on top with sharp knife or scissors - let rise till double size.
Bake @ 350° - 20 - 25 mins. - when cooled - fill cross with icing.

Poppy Seed Bread
Use Cinnamon Bun Dough

2 cups	**poppy seed (1 lb.)**	**1**	**egg - unbeaten**
1 1/2 cups	**milk**	**4 tbsp.**	**cream of wheat**
3/4 cup	**sugar**		

In a saucepan combine poppy seed and milk - cook slowly till milk is absorbed.
Stir in sugar - continue to cook - approx. 15 mins. - mixture will be quite thin.
Cool - stir in the egg - set aside.

Cook cream of wheat according to pkg. instructions for single serving (4 tbsp.) cool.
Combine cream of wheat and poppy seed mixture.

Roll out a piece of dough 8x12" x1" thick on floured surface.
Spread on poppy seed mix to within 1" of edge - 1/4" thick.
Roll up jelly roll fashion starting at the 8" side.
Pinch ends together - place in a greased loaf pan - seam side down.

Let rise to the top of pan - prick loaf with a meat fork several times to release air pockets.
Let rise another 1/2 hour.

Bake @ 350° till brown - approx. 25 mins.. Remove from oven - lay pan on its side on cooling rack.
After 10 - 15 mins. remove from pan - cool complete.

VARIATION: Cinnamon Bread

In place of poppy seed filling - spread dough with a thin layer of margarine - sprinkle generously with sugar and cinnamon.

At Christmas time these breads are served often.

Itterman's Paska

Traditional Easter Bread

2 cups	light cream	1 1/2 cups	sugar
2 cups	milk	1 /2 tsp.	salt
2 tbsp.	yeast	1 1/2 tbsp.	lemon juice
1 cup	butter or margarine	12 - 13 cups	flour
1 tbsp.	lard	1 tbsp.	oil
5	eggs - well beaten		
	grated rind of one large orange		
	chopped almonds or raisins opt.		

Into half a cup of luke warm water - place yeast with 1 tsp. sugar.
Let rest 10 mins. Heat milk and cream - DO NOT BOIL.

In mixer bowl cream together butter - lard and oil - add sugar and eggs.
beat well - add salt - lemon juice and orange rind.
Stir in the yeast mixture with 4 cups flour - beat well.
Add 6 cups more flour with almonds and raisins.
Knead approx. 10 mins. - working in extra flour if needed to make a soft
dough that forms into a big ball.
Dough should come away from sides of bowl and not stick to hands.

Cover with plastic and a towel over top to keep dough warm.
Let rise 1 hour - punch down - cover - let rise 45 mins. punch down.
Repeat the 45 min. - rising.

Prepare pans: Deep round pans. Cut down coffee cans to 5" - makes
interesting loaves. Grease generously with lard. Shape dough into a
ball that will fit the pan being used - press into pan - 1/3 full.
Cover with plastic - let rise till double size - remove plastic carefully.

Bake @ 350° - 30 - 40 mins. - depending on size of pan - should be
brown on top. IF NOT FIRM ON SIDES AND BOTTOM - BAKE A
LITTLE LONGER.
To test for DONENESS - loaf should seem loosened from the pan.

Remove from pan - cool on racks completely.
Before serving - frost with a thin frosting so it runs down sides.
Decorate with cake sprinkles.

Frosting:	1 cup	powdered/icing sugar	2 tsps. butter
	1/2 tsp.	vanilla	
		milk enough for spreading consistancy	
NOTE:	These breads freeze well.		

116

Notes:

Crowning Glories

Desserts
Pudding

Decadent Apricot Cheesecake

No bake crust:

1/2 cup	butter or margarine
1/3 cup	sugar
1 1/2 cup	graham wafer crumbs

Melt butter - stir in the sugar and crumbs - mix well.
Set 2 tbsp. aside (reserve) - press remainder into a spring form pan. Chill.

Filling:

2-14 oz. cans	apricot halves - drained - reserve syrup
1 env.	unflavoured gelatine
2-8 oz. pkgs.	cream cheese - softened
1-14 oz can	sweetened - condensed milk
2/3 cup	nutra whip or whipping cream - whipped

Combine 1/2 cup of reserve syrup with gelatine in a saucepan. Stir over low heat until gelatine dissolves.

Reserve 3-4 apricots for garnish - blend the remainder in a blender till smooth - add to the gelatine mix - stir and set aside.

In a large bowl beat cream cheese till smooth - mix in milk and lemon juice. Stir in the apricot gelatine mixture - fold in the whipped topping. Gently pour into pan over crumb base.

Garnish with reserve apricots. Spoon glaze over (see below).

Glaze:

Cook together over low heat until thick and clear.
1/2 cup reserve syrup and 1 tsp. corn starch.

Mint leaves may be added to apricot clusters for additional garnish.
Sprinkle reserve crumbs around the edge of cake using finger tips.
Chill for 3 hours.

Family Hint:

   Serves 12 but it doesn't last long with a family of four.

Cheesecake

1/2 cup	butter or margarine	1/4 tsp.	vanilla (opt.)
1/3 cup	sugar	1 cup	flour
1 tsp.	grated lemon zest		

<u>Crust:</u>   Combine together flour - sugar and lemon zest.
Cut in butter - make a crumbly dough mix.
Pat into bottom of a 9" spring form pan.
Bake @ 375° for 10 mins..
Cool while preparing the filling.

Filling

2-8oz. pkg.	cream cheese	1 cup	sugar
3 tbsp.	flour	1/2 tsp.	vanilla
1 tbsp.	corn starch	1/4 tsp.	lemon juice
3	eggs	1/4 cup	sour cream
	(room temperature)		

In a mixer bowl beat cream cheese till smooth - add flour and corn starch. Add sugar - beat till light and fluffy. Add vanilla and lemon juice - beat again.

Add eggs one at a time with mixer on low speed. Beat 2 mins. between each addition - stir in sour cream gently. Place cheese mixture on pre-baked crust.

<u>Baking instructions:</u>
Place a pan of hot water on lower shelf of oven directly under cheese cake.
Oven @ 325°   - Bake for 15 mins.
Lower heat to 250° - Bake for 15 mins.
Lower heat to 200° - Bake for 2 hours

Turn off oven - leave cheesecake in oven for 2 hours. Remove from oven - immediately place in refrigerator to cool completely. *Do not cover cheese cake* with foil or plastic wrap. Cover with cardboard or store in a cake box - in refrigerator - leave overnight before serving.
Serve with whipped cream - strawberries - raspberries - blueberries etc.

Caramel - Apple Raisin Dessert

If you can't make mothers strudel - try this - the taste and smell - oh-so-good.

Pie pastry for a double crust pie - 9" or 10" pie plate.

1/2 cup	raisins	2 tbsp.	fruit juice - choice
1/4 cup	butter	1 cup	pecan halves
2/3 cup	brown sugar	6 lge.	apples - peeled-sliced
2 tbsp.	lemon juice	1 tbsp.	flour
1/2 cup	white sugar	1 tsp.	cinnamon
1/8 tsp.	nutmeg		pinch of salt

Soak raisins with fruit juice a couple of hours.

Roll out dough for 2 pie crusts - set aside.

Spread butter over bottom and up sides of pie pan. Press pecans - round side down - evenly on sides and bottom of buttered pan. Sprinkle brown sugar over the nuts - (will create a caramel sauce).

Place carefully one pie crust over nuts and up the sides (as for normal pie shell).

Combine in a bowl - raisins - apples - white sugar - flour - lemon juice and spices. Put mixture into prepared pie pan - moisten edge of first pie shell - place the 2nd unbaked pie shell on top (moisture helps seal edges when crimping) seal well. Crimp edge - prick top crust with fork (steam vent).

Bake @ 450° - 10 mins. - reduce heat to 350° - 40 mins or nicely browned.

Cool pie on rack approximately 5 mins. - invert pie on nice serving plate - large enough for caramel sauce to flow (very hot).
Cool - serve plain - with whipped cream or ice cream.

German Torte

1/4 cup	soft butter	1 cup	flour
1	egg slightly beaten	2 tbsp.	milk
1 tsp.	baking powder	1 env.	OTKER pudding
1/8 tsp.	salt		powder
	rind of 1/2 lemon	3/4 cup	unsalted butter
1 cup	sugar - divided	1 tbsp.	corn starch

Mix together soft butter - egg - baking powder - salt - 1/2 cup of sugar - flour - milk and lemon rind. Make a soft dough - divide into 3 portions.

Line 3 layer cake pans with waxed paper - pat dough portions into each pan. Prick with fork.

Bake @ 350° - 15 mins. Remove from oven.

Gently run a knife blade around edge to loosen - turn out on rack - remove paper.

Buttercream Filling:

Prepare envelope of pudding powder as to pkg. directions plus adding remainder 1/2 cup of sugar and corn starch.
Cover pudding with plastic wrap so no skin forms on top during the cooling time. Stir pudding once as it cools.

When pudding is cooled to room temperature - complete the buttercream filling by adding the unsalted butter in small portions. Beat well after each addition - as this makes a difference.

Assemble torte by spreading buttercream between layers as you stack them on a nice serving plate. Frost top and sides with buttercream - using a decorator tube you can put decorative designs on top using the same Buttercream filling. Chocolate Curls - opt. (see That Extra Touch).

Cut serving pieces small as this is very rich. This torte should be prepared one day before serving. Keep refrigerated.

Remove from refrigerator - 2 hours before serving time.

Strawberry Short Cake

3 cups	flour	1 cup	sour milk
2/3 cups	brown sugar		(add 1 tsp. vinegar to
1 cup	butter or margarine		make milk sour)
1/2 tsp.	salt	1	egg beaten
1 tsp.	soda	1/2 cup	chopped walnuts
	strawberries		whipped cream

Make crumb mixture of flour, sugar, salt and margarine. Reserve one cupful of crumbs for the top.
Combine sour milk - egg and soda. Add the milk mixture to the crumb mixture - stir only enough to moisten.

Put into 3 greased 9" round pans. Add 1/2 cup chopped walnuts to the reserve crumb mixture and sprinkle evenly over the 3 pans.

Bake @ 350° for 15 - 20 mins. Test - do not over bake.

To serve - cut cake into serving size pieces and top with either sweetened fresh or frozen strawberries and a spoon of whipped cream.
* Extra cakes may be frozen.

Lemon Jello Dessert

28 single	graham wafers - crushed
1 cup	sugar
1/2 cup	melted margarine
1-3 oz.	strawberry jello
1-6 oz.	lemon pie filling
1 1/2 cup	whipping cream - whipped

Combine wafers, sugar and margarine for crust - reserve 1/2 cup for topping. Press into a 9x13" pan.
Prepare strawberry jello - as pkg. directions. Let set partially - spoon over base. Prepare lemon pie filling as pkg. directions - cool partially - spread over red jello.
Cool completely - top with sweetened whipped cream and reserve crumbs.

Banana Split Dessert

2 cups	graham cracker crumbs
1/4 cup	sugar
1 cup	margarine -divided
2	eggs
2 cups	powdered/icing sugar
3 - 5	bananas - sliced
1-14 oz. can	crushed pineapple - well drained
1 lge.	Cool Whip
3/4 cup	chopped nuts - pecans or walnuts
1 small jar	maraschino cherries - drained and chopped

Melt 1/2 cup margarine - combine with crumbs and 1/4 cup of sugar. Place in a 9x13" pan.

Combine other 1/2 cup margarine - eggs and powdered/icing sugar. Whip mixture for approximately 6 minutes (until very smooth) and spread over crumb mixture.

Place sliced bananas over mixture and top with pineapple. Spread Cool-Whip over pineapple and sprinkle nuts and cherries over all. Refrigerate over night.

VARIATION: Drizzle chocolate sauce over individual servings.

Cherry Cheesecake Supreme

1/2 cup	margarine - melted	1 cup	sugar
1/4 cup	sugar	8 oz.	cream cheese (soft)
2 cups	graham wafer crumbs	1 can	cherry pie filling
1 env.	Dream Whip - prepared		

Mix together margarine - 1/4 cup sugar and wafer crumbs. Press into a 9x9" pan.

Cream together cream cheese and 1 cup sugar. Stir into Dream Whip - put on wafer base - top with pie filling.
Chill one hour or longer - serves 10.

Rhubarb Meringue Dessert

Large Dessert - Delicious

<u>Base:</u> **Combine together -**
- **1 cup**   margarine (part butter)
- **2 cups**   flour
- **4 tbsp.**   sugar

Press into a 9x13" pan - bake for 20 mins. @ 325°.

<u>Filling:</u>
- **6**   eggs (separated)
- **2 1/2 cups** sugar
- **4 tbsp.**   flour
- **1 cup**   coffee cream or evaporated milk
- **6 cups**   cut up rhubarb - cut in 1/2 inch pieces

In saucepan combine sugar and flour - add 6 egg yolks (beaten).
Add coffee cream and rhubarb. Place on medium heat - boil
together till thick and clear, stirring often. Spoon mixture over
baked base.

<u>Topping:</u>
- **6**   egg whites
- **1/2 tsp.**   cream of tartar
- **3/4 cup**   sugar

In mixer bowl place egg whites and cream of tartar. Beat until
frothy - gradually add sugar (beat 8-10 mins.). Beat until stiff as
for meringue - spoon over rhubarb layer to edges of pan. Bake @
350° - 20 mins..

*Love is like an ocean - always there - always
different.*

French Vanilla Torte

1 lge.	instant french vanilla pudding (or vanilla) 6 serving size
1 lge.	Cool Whip
	whole graham wafers

Prepare pudding as per pkg. instructions using only 2 1/2 cups milk.
Let set 4 - 5 mins..

Line 9 x 13" pan with graham wafers.

Stir Cool Whip into pudding mixture until blended. Spread on top of the graham wafer crackers.

Top pudding mixture with another layer of graham wafers.

Spread chocolate icing over wafers. (See Frostings)
Refrigerate overnight.

Supreme Cherry Bombe

Crust:

1 1/3 cups	chocolate wafer crumbs	1/4 cup	sugar
		1/3 cup	butter or margarine

Melt margarine - combine with wafer crumbs and sugar.
Press into bottom and sides of a 9" pie pan. Bake @ 350° - 10 mins.. Cool.

Filling:

1-8 oz. pkg.	cream cheese	1 sm.	Cool Whip
1 cup	powdered/icing sugar		chopped pecans
1-19 oz. can	cherry pie filling		chocolate topping

Mix cream cheese and sugar together. Blend cherry pie filling and half of the Cool Whip into cream cheese mixture. Spread onto prepared crust. Top with remainder of Cool Whip - garnish with chopped pecans. Drizzle with chocolate topping (opt.).
NOTE: Low fat cream cheese and cool whip works very well.

Triffle

1	sponge cake or 2 small sized jelly rolls
1 lge. pkg.	vanilla pudding - cooked
1 cup	whipping cream - whipped
1 pkg.	strawberries - with juice
1 can	peach slices - drained
1/2 cup	orange juice
	raspberry jam

Prepare pudding as per pkg. directions. Cover with plastic wrap. Set aside to cool.

In a lge. clear glass serving bowl - place pieces of sponge cake or jelly roll slices over the bottom and up the sides of the bowl. Spread raspberry jam over cake and sprinkle with orange juice. Arrange peach slices over this - then strawberries. Spread the cooled pudding over the fruit.

Top with whipped cream - garnish with fresh fruit of choice. Chill 4 hrs. or overnight.

NOTE: This can be done in layers.

Peanut Buster Parfait

1 1/3 cups   **chocolate baking crumbs**
1/3 cup   **butter or margarine**
2 tbsp.   **sugar**

Mix together - press into a 9x13" pan-bake @ 325° for 5 mins..
Cool.

2 litres   **ice cream**
               (softened) = 8 cups
2 cups   **spanish or salted peanuts**
2/3 cup   **chocolate chips**
2/3 cup   **powdered/icing sugar**
1/4 cup   **margarine**
1 1/2 cups   **evaporated milk**

Spread softened ice cream over crumb base - sprinkle nuts over
this - freeze.

In a saucepan over med. heat combine chocolate chips - sugar -
margarine and milk. Bring to a boil for 7 mins. - spoon over
peanuts - return to freezer.

When serving - decorate each slice with a maraschino cherry.

Chocolate Cream Roll

3	eggs	1/4 cup	cocoa (sifted)
1 cup	sugar	1 cup	cake flour
1/3 cup	cold coffee	1 tsp.	baking powder
1 tsp.	vanilla	1/4 tsp.	salt
			powdered/icing sugar

Beat eggs till foamy and lemon colored. Gradually add sugar, beat well - add coffee and vanilla. Combine dry ingredients - stir and gently fold into batter.

Oil and line a 10"x14" pan with a double layer of waxed paper, and oil again. Spread batter in pan.

Bake @ 375° for 12 - 15 mins.. Watch closely - this is baked when it begins to pull away from sides .

NOTE: Have a tea towel spread out on counter, which has been sprinkled with powdered/icing sugar. When baked - immediately invert pan on towel. Pull off waxed paper - trim edges with a sharp knife if needed.

Starting at the short side roll up towel and cake together, jellyroll style - leave on rack to cool. When thoroughly cooled, unroll and fill with Coffee Cream Filling and ice with Chocolate Satin Frosting; (listed under frostings).

VARIATION: To make a plain jelly roll - omit cocoa - use water in place of coffee. Fill with whipped cream/softened ice cream/jam/lemon cream (see frostings). Garnish with strawberries - sprinkle with icing sugar.

When God measures man He puts the measuring tape around the heart; not around the head.

Chocolate Mousse Dessert

2	eggs	3/4 cup	flour
1/2 cup	oil	1/4 cup	cocoa - sifted
1 cup	sugar	1 tsp.	baking powder
1 cup	chocolate chips	1/8 tsp.	salt
1/2 cup	chopped nuts		

In a bowl beat together eggs - oil and sugar till fluffy.

Stir dry ingredients together - add to egg mixture. Stir in chocolate chips and nuts.

Pour into a greased 9" springform pan.
Bake @ 350° for 25 mins.. Cool - remove from pan.

Topping:

1 8 oz.pkg.	cream cheese	2 tsp.	powdered/icing sugar
1/2 cup	whipping cream	1/2 tsp.	almond flavoring

Combine whipping cream - icing sugar and flavorings; whip till thickened. Set aside.

Beat cream cheese thoroughly - stir in cream - spread over base.

Garnish with chocolate curls or sliced toasted almonds.
Refrigerate before serving - serves approximately 12.

Often we stand at lifes crossroads and view what we think is the end, but God has a bigger vision and He tells us its only a bend.

Layered Mousse Dessert

Crust:

2 1/2 cups   graham wafer crumbs
1/2 cup   butter or margarine - melted
1/2 cup   sugar

Mix together and press into 9 x13" pan. Chill.

Filling:

1 pkg.	chocolate mousse	2 tbsp.	Nestle's Quick
1 pkg.	vanilla mousse	1/2 cup	cold milk
1 env.	Dream Whip		grated chocolate or chips

Mix chocolate mousse as to pkg. directions - spread over crust. Chill.

Mix vanilla mousse as to pkg. directions - spread over chocolate layer. Chill.

Beat together Dream Whip - Nestle's Quick and milk at high speed until peaks form and it is light and fluffy. Spread over vanilla layer.

Garnish with chocolate shavings - chill well before serving.

Give some people an inch, and they think they are rulers.

Apple Coffee Cake Dessert

Topping:

3/4 cup	brown sugar	3 tbsp.	flour
1 tsp.	cinnamon	1/2 cup	chopped nuts
3	apples (peeled & diced)		(optional)

Combine and set aside.

Cake Batter:

1/2 cup	butter or margarine	2 tsp.	baking powder
1 cup	sugar	1 1/4 cups	flour
2	eggs	1/2 tsp.	salt
1 tsp.	vanilla	1/2 cup	sour milk or buttermilk

Cream butter and sugar together - add eggs and vanilla. Beat well.

Combine flour - baking powder and salt. Add alternately with the milk to the creamed mixture - beat until smooth.

Place batter into a greased 9" square or round pan. Sprinkle with prepared topping.

Bake @ 350° for 35 - 40 mins..
Cut into squares - serve warm with ice cream or whipped cream.

VARIATION: Substitute apples with other fruit - peaches, etc..

Middle age is when your narrow waist and broad mind change places.

132

Cool Fruit Pizza or Tarts

Crust:

1 cup	flour	2 tbsp.	powdered/icing sugar
1/4 cup	brown sugar	1/2 cup	butter or margarine (room temp.)

Mix ingredients until they stick together.
Pat mixture into a pizza pan with fingers or into tart pans slightly up sides.

Bake @ 350° for 10 - 15 mins. or until browned lightly - (less for tarts). Cool.

Filling:

3 oz.	cream cheese - softened		
1/3 cup	sugar	3/4 cup	whipping cream
1/2 cup	apple jelly - melted	1 tsp.	vanilla
	assorted fruits		

Beat together cheese - sugar and vanilla till smooth.
Whip cream - combine with cheese mix - spread over crust.

Arrange fruits of choice in desired fashion - eg. strawberries - sliced peaches - blueberries - raspberries - kiwi - bananas - grapes etc.

Drizzle melted jelly over the top - spread lightly - refrigerate.

<u>Optional Glaze</u>

Cook together	1/2 cup	orange juice
till medium thick.	1/2 cup	sugar
	1/2 cup	water
	1 1/2 tbsp.	corn starch

Cool and spread over top.

Fruit Coctail Dessert

1 3/4 cup	sugar	1/4 tsp.	salt
2 cups	flour	1-14 oz. can	fruit cocktail
2 tsp.	soda	3/4 cup	brown sugar
2	eggs - beaten	3/4 cup	chopped nuts
			walnuts or pecans

Combine sugar - flour - soda - eggs - salt and fruit coctail with juice.
Stir well. Pour into a greased and floured 9 x 13" pan or bundt pan.

Combine brown sugar and nuts. Sprinkle over top.
Bake at 350° for 45 mins.. Serve warm or cool with ice cream or whipped cream.

VARIATION: **Bundt Cake Sauce**

1/2 cup	butter or margarine
3/4 cup	sugar
1/2 cup	cream

Combine ingredients in saucepan - bring to a boil for 1 min.. Remove from heat - stir in 1/2 tsp. vanilla. Spoon sauce over warm cake while still in bundt pan. Let sit 20 min. for flavors to blend before removing from pan. Invert on serving platter.

134

Christmas Pudding

This pudding needs to steam for 3 hrs.

1/2 cup	butter	2 cups	flour
1 cup	sugar	1/2 tsp.	allspice
1	egg	1/2 tsp.	salt
1 tbsp.	molasses	1 tsp.	soda
2 cup	raisins	1/2 tsp.	cinnamon
1 cup	grated raw carrots		
1 cup	grated raw potatoes		

Prepare raisins - place in a bowl - cover with hot water and soak 30 min.. Drain well - place on paper towel to dry. (This will plump raisins.)

Prepare grated raw carrots and potatoes in a food processor.

Cream together butter - sugar and egg. Combine dry ingredients and add to creamed mixture along with carrots and potatoes. Stir in molasses and raisins.

Place batter in quart jars - fill only 1/2 full. Place jars in food canner or pot of similar size. Jars need to be immersed in water up to the metal ring. Bring water to an almost boil - cover and keep at a constant simmer for 3 hrs. Yield - 3 - 4 quarts.
Serve pudding hot with caramel sauce.

NOTE: Pudding may be made days ahead and kept if jars seal well. To reheat place jars in a pot of hot water on stove until completely warmed for serving.

Caramel Sauce:
4 tbsp.   corn starch
3 tbsp.   cold water
Place in a saucepan and mix together.

2 cups	hot water	1 tbsp.	butter
1/2 tsp.	salt	1 tsp.	vanilla or rum
1 cup	brown sugar (packed)		flavoring

Add water - salt and sugar to corn starch mixture. Bring to a boil and stir while sauce thickens. Remove from heat - add butter and flavoring.

NOTE: This is a must at Christmas for our family.

Bread Pudding

2 cups	milk		1/4 tsp.	salt
2 cups	soft bread crumbs		1/3 cup	raisins
1 tbsp.	margarine		2	eggs - beaten
1/4 cup	sugar			

In a saucepan heat milk - add margarine and crumbs.

In a bowl place eggs - sugar - salt and raisins. Slowly stir into the hot mixture. Place batter in a greased baking dish - then set into a pan containing 1" of water.
Bake @ 350° - 1 hr. or until set.

Serve with cream or sauce.

NOTE: This pudding is delicious if fruits are added as a centre layer such as peaches or blueberries.

Vanilla Sauce:
Combine 1/3 cup vanilla instant pudding with 3 cups of milk. Beat on low speed for 2 min. until blended.

Creamy Rice Pudding

1/2 cup	rice		1	egg - beaten
1/4 cup	raisins		1/4 cup	milk
1/4 tsp.	salt		1/3 cup	sugar
1 1/2 cups	water		1 tsp.	vanilla
1 cup	milk			

In a saucepan combine rice - salt - raisins and water. Bring to a boil over med. heat. Cover - reduce heat to simmer and cook 20 mins. stirring often.
Add 1 cup milk - cook 10 minutes longer.

In a bowl mix together egg - 1/4 cup milk - sugar and vanilla. Add to the cooked rice - cook till slightly thickened stirring constantly. Yield - 4 servings.

Saucy Raisin Pudding

2 1/2 cups	boiling water	1 cup	brown sugar
2 tbsp.	margarine		

Combine together in a large baking dish.

In a bowl mix together:

1 tbsp.	margarine	1 cup	flour
1/2 cup	brown sugar	1/2 cup	milk
2 tsp.	baking powder	1 tsp.	vanilla
1/2 tsp.	soda	1/2 cup	raisins

Mix together - drop into sauce by spoonfuls.
Bake @ 350° - 30 - 40 mins.. Sauce will rise to the top.
Serve with cream.

Chocolate Fudge Pudding

Makes it's own sauce.

1 cup	flour	2 tbsp.	oil
2 tsp.	baking powder	1 tsp.	vanilla
1/2 tsp.	salt	1/2 cup	chopped nuts
3/4 cup	white sugar	1 cup	brown sugar
3 tbsp.	cocoa	1/4 cup	cocoa
1/2 cup	milk	2 cups	hot water

Mix together flour - baking powder - salt - white sugar and 3 tbsp. cocoa. Add milk - oil and vanilla - blend together well. Stir in walnuts.

Pour into an 8x8" pan.

Combine brown sugar and 1/4 cup cocoa - sprinkle over batter.

Slowly pour hot water over the mix in pan - bake @ 350° - 40 - 50 mins..

Notes:

That Extra Touch

Frostings - Fillings
Sweet Sauces
Savory Sauces
Gravies - Marinades

Pudding Icing

1 env.	Dream Whip
1 1/2 cups	milk
1-4 oz. pkg.	vanilla instant pudding

Mix together in a mixer bowl - beat until stiff. (May need to double recipe.)

Royal Icing

4 cups	powdered/icing sugar
1/2 tsp.	cream of tartar
3	egg whites - room temperature

Beat in a mixer on high speed - 7 - 10 mins.
Used for cake decorating purposes - Yield 2 1/2 cups.

Caramel Icing

1/2 cup	butter
1/2 cup	brown sugar - packed
4 tbsp.	milk or half & half
2 cups	powdered/icing sugar
1 tsp.	vanilla

In a saucepan melt butter - add sugar - stir over low heat for 2 mins.
Add milk - continue stirring until it begins to bubble. Remove from heat.

With mixer -beat in powdered/icing sugar and vanilla.

More powdered/icing sugar may be needed for desired consistency.
If icing becomes to thick - add a few drops of hot water to thin.

Coffee Whip Icing

1 cup	white sugar	1 tbsp.	corn syrup
1/2 cup	brown sugar	1/4 tsp.	cream of tartar
2/3 cup	strong coffee	2	egg whites
1 tsp.	vanilla		

In a saucepan cook together coffee - white sugar and syrup to thread stage or till it strings from a fork.

Pour slowly into stiffly beaten egg whites to which cream of tartar has been added.

Beat until it forms peaks - add vanilla - put on cooled cake.

VARIATION:

<u>Sea Foam Icing:</u> Substitute white sugar with brown - coffee with water.

<u>White Icing:</u> Substitute brown sugar with white.

Cream Cheese Icing

1/2 cup	margarine or butter	1-8 oz. pkg.	cream cheese
2 tsp.	vanilla	4 cups	powdered/
1 tbsp.	water		icing sugar

Cream together butter and cream cheese. Add vanilla - water and sugar - beat till fluffy.

VARIATION: Chocolate Cream Cheese Icing

Substitute 1/4 cup cocoa for 1/4 cup powdered/icing sugar.

White / Chocolate / Mocha Icing

1/2 cup	margarine	3 cups	powdered/icing sugar
3 tbsp.	water	1 tsp.	vanilla

Cream margarine - add sugar - vanilla and water.
Beat well - beating will make it fluffy.
If icing is too thick add a little extra water.

VARIATION:

Chocolate: Add 3 tbsp. sifted cocoa.
Mocha: Same as chocolate plus 1/2 tsp. instant coffee
             granules or powder.

Lemon Cream Filling

4	egg yolks - slightly beaten	1/2 cup	sugar
5 tbsp.	lemon juice	1 tbsp.	lemon rind
1 tbsp.	butter		(finely grated)

In a saucepan combine all ingredients - except butter.

Cook over low heat till thickened - remove from heat.
Stir in butter - cover with plastic wrap - let cool.

Use to fill tart shells or meringues.

VARIATION: Combine and whip 1 cup whipping cream with 2
tbsp. powdered sugar until thickened or prepare 1 envelope of
Dream Whip. Blend into lemon filling.

Coffee Cream Filling

Used for Chocolate Cream Roll

2 tsp.	instant coffee granules
1 1/2 cup	whipping cream - divided
1/2 cup	powdered/icing sugar

Dissolve coffee granules in 1/4 cup of the cream. Add rest of cream - sugar - beat till stiff.
Spread on unrolled chocolate roll - roll up carefully.

Place on to a serving plate or tray - seam side down. A doily may be placed on tray before placing chocolate roll.

Before frosting tuck some wax paper over exposed edges of doily to keep clean. Remove gently after frosting is applied.

Chocolate Satin Frosting

3 sq.	semi-sweet chocolate or 1/2 cup chocolate chips
1/8 cup	strong coffee
1/2 cup	butter or margarine - softened
1/3 cup	white syrup
2	egg yolks

Melt chocolate in coffee in microwave or over low heat - cool.
In a bowl beat butter - stir in cooled chocolate mixture.
Add syrup - egg yolks - beat till smooth.

NOTE: This frosting is used on the Chocolate Cream Roll - see desserts - Enjoy!

Chocolate Sauce

1/2 cup	butter or margarine	1 tbsp.	instant coffee granules/powder
2 cups	semi-sweet chocolate chips	2 cups	powdered/ icing sugar
1/4 tsp.	salt - scant	1 cup	hot water
3 tsp.	vanilla	1 cup	light corn syrup

Place butter - chocolate chips - coffee - salt and vanilla in a saucepan.
Over medium heat stir until smooth - remove from heat.
Beat in sugar - water and syrup.
If it becomes lumpy - place in a blender until smooth.

Makes approx. 4 cups and will keep in the fridge.
May be heated in microwave to serve hot over ice cream.

Caramel Sauce

Version #1

| 1/2 cup | white sugar | 1/2 cup | brown sugar |
| 1/2 cup | butter | 1/2 cup | whipping cream |

Version #2

| 1 cup | packed brown sugar | 1 cup | corn syrup |
| 1/4 cup | margarine | | |

Combine all ingredients in a small saucepan.
Bring to a boil - cook one minute - serve with cake or pudding.

Easy Caramel Sauce

Place in a saucepan - 28 Kraft caramels with 1/2 cup water.
Heat and stir constantly till melted and smooth - Yield 1 cup.

Croutons

4 slices	**French Bread**	**1/2 tsp.**	**garlic powder**
	1/2" thick	**1/2 tsp.**	**oregano (opt.)**
1/4 cup	**margarine or butter**	**1/2 tsp.**	**thyme (opt.)**
		1/2 tsp.	**basil (opt.)**

Cut bread slices into 3/4" cubes.

In large skillet melt butter - remove from heat - add garlic and spices.
Add bread cubes - stir to coat well.

Spread bread cubes in a single layer on shallow baking sheet.
Place into a pre-heated 300° oven for 10 mins. - stir.
Bake for another 5 mins. or till bread cubes are dry and crisp.
Makes about 2 cups.

NOTE: Other types of bread may be used.
Variety croutons are made by using parmesan cheese or dill weed.

Applesauce

4	**apples - cut in chunks**
1/2 cup	**water**
	juice of 1/2 lemon
1/2 cup	**sugar**
1/2 tsp.	**cinnamon**

In a microwave dish - place apples - water and lemon juice.
Mix together sugar and cinnamon - add to apple mixture.
Cook - uncovered for 5 mins. - stir - microwave 5 mins. more.

Use a potato masher to make a coarse mixture.

Allow applesauce to cool - cover and refrigerate.

Beef Marinade

1/2 cup	wine vinegar	1 1/2 cups	vegetable oil
1/3 cup	lemon juice	3/4 cup	soya sauce
2	cloves garlic (crushed)	1/4 cup	worcestershire sauce
2 tsp.	salt		
1 tsp.	thyme	2 tbsp.	pepper
1 tsp.	parsley flakes	2 tbsp.	horseradish(opt.)
2 tbsp.	dry/dijon mustard		

Combine all ingredients - stir to blend. Pour over meat - turn occasionally.
Marinate at least 4 hrs. or overnight.

VARIATION: Basic Marinade

Mix together - 2 parts oil - 1 part vinegar - 1 minced garlic or onion.
Salt and pepper - herbs and spices to taste.

Pork Marinade

1/4 cup	lemon juice	1/2 cup	melted honey or brown sugar
1/2 cup	soya sauce		
1/2 cup	cooking oil	2 tsp.	dry mustard
3 tsp.	ginger		
1	clove minced garlic		

Combine all ingredients - pour over meat - marinade 3 hrs. or more.
Excess marinade may be saved.

NOTE: Marinades add seasoning - bring out natural flavors - supplies fat to meats lacking natural oils - tenderizes bysoftening tough fibre in the meat. Marinades can be used for basting meats.

Chicken Marinade

1/2 cup	vinegar	1 tsp.	worcestershire
1/3 cup	vegetable oil		sauce
3/4 tsp.	salt	1 sm.	onion - grated
1/2 tsp.	paprika	2 tsp.	garlic salt or juice
1/2 cup	tomato juice or ketchup		

Combine all ingredients - pour over chicken - marinade 4 hrs. or overnight.

VARIATION:
Juice and zest of 1/2 lemon and 1/2 orange
1/4 cup Dijon mustard   1/4 cup melted honey

Combine - pour over chicken - marinate 4 hrs. or overnight.

Marinade for Salmon

1 tsp.	sesame oil	1/2 cup	soya sauce
2 cloves	garlic - chopped	1 tsp.	fresh ground ginger

Marinade salmon for several hours. Cook on grill allowing approx. ten minutes per inch of thickness. This is delicious.

Tartar Sauce

1/3 cup	mayonnaise	1/3 cup	creamed
1/3 cup	dairy sour cream		horseradish
1/4 tsp.	dried celery leaves crushed	1 tsp.	dill seed
		1 tsp.	sugar
2-3 drops	hot pepper sauce		dash of pepper

Combine all ingredients and mix thoroughly. Refrigerate; keeps about one week. Makes approx. 1 cup.
VARIATION: Add one diced tomato.

White Sauce (Med.) Microwave

2 tbsp.	butter	2 tbsp.	flour
1/2 tsp.	salt	1 cup	milk

Microwave butter in bowl till melted - 30 sec.
Stir in flour and salt to make a smooth paste.
Add milk gradually - stirring constantly.
Microwave uncovered for 1 min. - stir well.
Cook 1 1/2 - 2 mins. - stirring every 30 seconds. Makes 1 cup.

VARIATION: Cheese Sauce
Add 1 cup grated cheddar cheese - stir till melted.
May be served over vegetables or potatoes.

Lemon Herb Sauce
Add: 1 tbsp. of combined herbs such as basil - dill - parsley etc.
Add: 1 tbsp. lemon juice
May be served with seafood or vegetables.

Quick Gravies

Onion Gravy
Combine: 1 pouch onion soup mix
                     2 tbsp. flour
Add - stir in: 2 cups cold water
Bring to a boil - simmer together.
May be used to pour over oven baked pork chops - last half hour
of baking.

Mushroom Gravy
In skillet saute: 1 small chopped onion in 2 tbsp. butter
Add: 1 can mushroom soup
                      1 can sliced mushrooms - undrained
                      3 tbsp. flour
                      1 1/4 cup half & half cream
                      1/2 tsp. parsley
                      1/2 tsp. lemon juice
Stir and cook until well blended and thickened.

Honey Mustard Sauce

Excellent served with ham. Microwave Method

1 cup	sugar	2	eggs
4 tsp.	dry mustard	1/2 cup	vinegar
		1 tsp.	honey

In a microwavable dish combine sugar and mustard.
Add eggs - beat well together - add vinegar - mix together.
Microwave on high 3 - 4 mins. Add honey - stir till melted.

Barbecue Sauce

2 cups	ketchup	1 tsp.	salt
1/2 cup	cider vinegar	2 tbsp.	oil
2	garlic cloves	2/3 cup	worcestershire
	crushed		sauce
	dash of cayenne pepper		

Blend all together - store in refrigerator.

Plum Sauce

1 1/2 tsp.	dry mustard	1 tbsp.	vegetable oil
1 1/2 tsp.	vinegar	1/2 cup	plum jam
			- no skins

Combine all ingredients - mix well.

Notes:

151

Versatile Dishes

Vegetables
Casseroles
Other

Scalloped Potatoes
(Pre-cooked)

6 med. size potatoes - cooked with skins on till fork tender. Drain - cool - remove skins - cut into small cubes. Put into a buttered oven proof casserole dish.

<u>Sauce:</u>   **Combine:**   **1 med.**   **onion - diced**
                              1 can   **mushroom soup**
                              1 cup   **milk**
                              1/2 cup   **Velveeta Cheese - cut up**

Place in saucepan and cook over med. heat until heated through.

Pour sauce over potatoes - sprinkle with parmesan cheese or crushed corn flakes.

Bake @ 350° approx. 45 mins. or until well heated through.

VARIATION: These potatoes may be peeled - sliced and pre-boiled for a quicker way. Use the same method and sauce. For an interesting topping - mix together dry fine bread crumbs with melted butter and crushed garlic. So good!

Harvard Beets

1 tbsp.	**corn starch**	**1/2 cup**	**sugar**
1/2 cup	**vinegar**	**1/2 tsp.**	**salt**
1/2 tbsp.	**butter**		

3 cups of cooked small beets - diced - drained (reserve juice)

Combine ingredients (except beets) in a saucepan - cook until smooth and thickened. If too thick - use some of reserved juice to thin.
Heat beets separately (in micro). Pour hot sauce over beets and serve.

VARIATION: <u>Sauce:</u> 1/3 cup sugar - 1 heaping tbsp. corn starch - 1 tbsp. butter - 1 cup orange juice - pinch of salt

Scalloped Potatoes

6 cups	peeled potatoes - thinly sliced	1/2 tsp.	pepper
1 med.	onion - chopped fine	5 tsp.	margarine or butter
1/4 cup	flour	2 cups	milk
2 tsp.	salt		

In microwave - heat milk and margarine only until melted - do not boil - set aside.

Combine flour - salt and pepper - set aside.
In a large greased casserole dish spread 1 cup of the sliced potatoes and some onion.
Sprinkle with 1 tbsp. flour mix - repeat in layers.
Pour milk and butter mixture over last layer of potatoes.

Milk should be to top of potatoes - but not completely covering them.
With spoon gently stir through potatoes - blending everything together.

Bake uncovered in 350° oven for 1 hr. - 1 hr. 15 mins. until lightly browned and milk absorbed - but still creamy. Do not over bake or potatoes will be dry.

Serves 4 - 6

NOTE: You may add more potatoes for extra servings - Just repeat above portions using approx. 1/2 cup milk for every cup of sliced potatoes. Baking time will have to be increased.

These cook up and run over easily so make sure your dish isn't too full or spread foil under to prevent a mess in the oven.

Broccoli Bake

4 cups	broccoli - bite size pieces
1 cup	grated med. cheese
1 can	mushroom soup
1/4 cup	milk
1/4 cup	salad dressing
1	egg - beaten
1/4 cup	margarine
1 1/2 cups	crushed Ritz crackers

Cut and cook broccoli till crunchy. Place in casserole dish. Sprinkle with cheese.

Blend together - soup - egg - milk - salad dressing . Pour over broccoli.

Mix margarine and cracker crumbs together - spread over top. Bake @350° - 45 mins..

VARIATION: Cauliflower may be used.

Corn on the Cob

Remove husks and silk.

In a large kettle - bring to boil enough water to cover corn. Gently drop in ears of corn - boil until tender (approx. 3 - 5 mins.). Serve with butter and salt.

<u>Microwave Method:</u>   After removing husks and silk - wrap each cob in paper towel or waxed paper. Microwave each cob 5 - 7 mins..

Scalloped Corn

1 1/2 cup	kernel corn (reserve liquid)	2	eggs-beaten
1/2 cup	half & half or evaporated milk	1/2 cup	buttered bread crumbs
2 tbsp.	butter		dash of pepper
2 tbsp.	flour		paprika
1 tsp.	salt		

Drain liquid from canned corn into a measuring cup. Add enough cream or evaporated milk to measure 1 cup. In a saucepan heat butter - add flour - salt and pepper. Stir until blended.

Slowly add liquid and cook stirring constantly until thickened. Remove from heat and add corn. Gradually add eggs stirring constantly.

Pour into a greased casserole dish. Top with buttered crumbs - sprinkle with paprika. Place in a shallow pan of water - bake @ 350° - 45 - 50 mins.. Serves 4.

Sweet and Sour Cabbage

1 cup	water	1/2 cup	vinegar
1 tsp.	salt	1/2 cup	sugar
1 med.	cabbage - finely shredded		

Place cabbage into a saucepan with water. Simmer until cabbage is tender - approx. 30 mins.. Drain well using a colander - return cabbage to pot.
In a bowl mix together vinegar - sugar and salt. Stir into cabbage until the sugar is dissolved. Adjust to taste if desired.
VARIATION: Chopped apple may be added and red or green cabbage may be used. This may be served hot or cold.

Oma usually had a jar of this in her refrigerator. This is excellent served with roast pork or pork chops!

Baked Onions

4 - 5   **med. onions - peeled and quartered**
            butter
            salt and pepper

Place onions in a greased baking dish - sprinkle with salt and pepper.
Dot with butter. Cover and bake @ 350° - 30 min. or till tender.
Great served at a B.B.Q. over baked potatoes.

Brown Baked Beans

2 14oz.cans	brown beans	2 tbsp.	molasses
1/2 cup	ketchup	1 tbsp.	prepared mustard
2/3 cup	brown sugar	1/4 cup	chopped green
1 med.	onion - chopped		pepper (opt.)
1/2 cup	barbecue sauce	1 1/2 tsp.	salt
		6 slices	bacon

Cut bacon slices into 1/2 " pieces. Fry or micro until cooked but not crisp. Combine all ingred. in a casserole dish or bean pot. Bake @ 350° - uncovered for 45 - 60 mins..

Yummy Yams
(Sweet Potatoes)

Wash and boil potatoes with skins on until almost tender.

Cool - peel and slice into 3/4 " thickness. Roll in flour. Place approx. 1/2 cup butter in skillet - when melted - place potatoes in skillet in a single layer. Sprinkle generously with brown sugar. Fry over low heat 1/2 to 3/4 hr. - uncovered. When nicely browned - turn over and fry other side.

Green Bean Mandarin

2 tbsp.	blanched almonds	1 tsp.	soya sauce
1 tbsp.	cooking oil	1 tsp.	sugar
1/2 cup	celery(coursly sliced or chopped)		
1/2 cup	bean liquid	2 tsp.	white vinegar
2 tsp.	dry chicken stock	2 tbsp.	corn starch
1 14oz.can	cut green beans- drain - (reserve liquid)	2 tbsp.	water

In a skillet - lightly brown almonds in oil. Add celery and saute for 2 mins.. Stir in 1/2 cup of reserved bean liquid - chicken stock - soya sauce - sugar and vinegar. Cover and simmer for 3 mins..

Add beans and cook till heated.

Combine water and corn starch till dissolved - stir into the bean mixture and heat until thickened.

Serves 4

Glazed Carrots

6-7 med.	carrots	2 tsp.	brown sugar
2 tbsp.	margarine		pinch of salt
	parsley (opt.)		

Scrub and peel carrots - cut in diagonal slices.

Place in saucepan - add water to cover - cook till tender.

Drain - add butter - salt and sugar.

Stir over low heat till carrots are coated.
Sprinkle with parsley.

Serves 4

Sliced Potato Bake

6-8	potatoes	1/4 tsp.	pepper
	- sliced thin	1/2 tsp.	dillweed
2	green onions		dry or fresh
	- chopped	1 1/2 tsp.	salt
2 tbsp.	margarine - melted		
	or oil		

Prepare potatoes - place in a bowl.
Toss with remaining ingredients - put into a baking dish.
Cover - bake 30 mins. @ 350° - uncover - bake 15 mins. - longer.

Microwave Method:
Cover and bake on high for 8 mins.
Stir and cook an additional 8 mins. or until cooked.

Hash Brown Bake

2 lbs.	frozen hash browns	2 cups	sour cream
	- slightly thawed	1 tsp.	salt
2 cans	mushroom soup	2 med.	onions
1/4 cup	butter or margarine - melted		- grated
2 cups	shredded cheddar cheese		

In a large bowl combine hash browns - cream - soup - butter - salt
- onion and cheese - mix well.

Reserve a little of the cheese to sprinkle over the top.
Spoon into a lightly greased or non-stick sprayed 9x13" baking
dish.

Bake @ 350° for 1 - 1 1/2 hours.

VARIATION: To add extra flavor - put a layer of ham chunks or
slices between potato layers. The sauce can be a light version if
you use 1 cup of sour cream with 3/4 cup of milk.

Stuffed Baked Potatoes

6	bakers potatoes	1/4-1/2 cup	hot milk
1/2 tsp.	salt	1 cup	grated cheddar
1/8 tsp.	pepper		cheese
2 tbsp.	butter	1 tbsp.	finely chopped
2/3 cup	sour cream		parsley/dill (opt.)
1/4 cup	green onion - chopped (opt.)		

Wash and bake potatoes with skins on in oven @ 375° - when cooked - remove from oven.
If potatoes are large - cut in half lengthwise.
If potatoes are smaller - slice only a portion off the top (lid).

Scoop out the inner potato using a spoon - place in a bowl.
Set shells aside - try not to break or crush them.

Mash potatoes well - add salt - pepper - butter - sour cream - grated cheese and hot milk.
Ingredients of choice may be added such as parsley - dill and green onion.
Refill potato shells with mashed potatoes in mounds. Destroy lids.

To serve - reheat in oven - garnish with grated cheese - bacon bits - green onion snips.

NOTE: These may be wrapped individually in foil and frozen without the garnish.

Whipped Potato Dish

10-12 med.	potatoes	1 tsp.	salt	
1/4 cup	butter or margarine		ground pepper	
1-8 oz. pkg.	cream cheese	1/2 tsp.	onion powder	
1 cup	sour cream	3 tbsp.	melted margarine	
1/2 cup	fine dry bread crumbs			
	choppted parsley (opt.)			

Peel and cook potatoes in salted boiling water until tender.
Drain and return to stove top briefly to dry up some moisture in pot.
Mash potatoes well with butter - add cheese - sour cream and seasonings.
Beat till creamy and smooth - spoon into a greased 2 qt. casserole.
Combine 3 tbsp. melted margarine with bread crumbs - sprinkle over top.
Bake uncovered @ 350° for 30 mins. or until hot.
Sprinkle with parsley if desired - 10 servings.

NOTE: These may be covered and refrigerated or frozen.
Remove from fridge - 1 1/2 hours before serving - if frozen - let thaw a couple of hours. Bake @ 350° - 45 - 55 mins.

Mexican Casserole

3	chicken breasts - cook and cut into chunks		
1 pkg.	tortillas - 1 lb. (corn or flour - tear into pieces)		
1 lb.	grated cheddar cheese	1/2 lb.	Jack cheese
1 can	cream of mushroom soup	1/2 cup	milk
1 can	cream of chicken soup	1 can	chili
8 oz.	taco sauce (salsa opt.)		without beans
1 sm. can	black olives - sliced	1 can	mushrooms
1 sm.	onion - chopped fine		drained

Mix soups - chili - salsa - olives - onions and milk together.
Layer into casserole - sauce - tortillas - chicken and cheese.
Always end with a cheese layer - bake @ 375° - 45 mins.

Kidney Bean Casserole

1-2 tins	kidney beans	1 1/2 lbs.	ground beef
1-28 oz.	stewed tomatoes	2 cans	tomato soup
1	onion - sliced	1/2 cup	water
	salt and pepper		potatoes
			potato chips

Peel and slice potatoes (amt. needed) layer in a greased
casserole dish. Sprinkle with salt and pepper.
Place a layer of kidney beans and tomatoes.
In fry pan - combine ground beef - onions - salt and pepper.
Brown and drain off juice. Put this mixture on top of tomatoes.
Mix tomato soup with water - pour over meat.
Cover - bake @ 350° for 2 - 2 1/2 hours.
Just before serving sprinkle with crushed potato chips.
May be served with baking powder biscuits.

Lazy Cabbage Rolls

1 lb.	lean ground beef	1 tsp.	salt
2 med.	onions chopped	3 cups	water
1 clove	garlic - minced	1 cup	rice
1-14 oz.	tomato sauce	1/4 tsp.	pepper
6 cups	shredded cabbage		

Combine and brown together - beef - onions - garlic - salt and
pepper. Stir in tomato sauce and water.
Bring to a boil - stir in rice - cover and simmer 30 mins.

Place 1/2 of the cabbage in greased baking dish.
Cover with 1/2 of the rice mixture - repeat layers.
Cover and bake @ 350° for 1 hour - Serves 4

To Serve: Top with heated tomato soup (undiluted) or sour
cream.

Canton Noodle Dish

1 tin	mushroom soup	1/4 cup	water
1 cup	celery - diced	1/4 cup	onion - chopped
2 cups	chow mein noodles	1-7.5 oz.	tin flaked tuna
1/2 cup	salted toasted cashews (optional)		orange sections (optional)

In baking dish combine together soup - water - celery- onions - tuna and noodles - toss lightly.
Bake @ 275° - 15 - 20 mins. (sprinkle nuts on top (opt.).
When serving - decorate with orange sections.

Lasagna

1 1/2 lb.	ground beef	1 tsp.	oregano
1-28 oz.	canned tomatoes	1 tsp.	basil
1-14 oz.	seasoned tomato sauce	1/2 tsp.	rosemary (ground)
2 cloves	garlic - minced	1 med.	onion - minced
8 oz. pkg.	lasagna noodles	1 tsp.	salt
8 oz.	shredded mozzarella cheese	2 tbsp.	sugar
		2 tbsp.	parsley flakes
1 1/2 cups	creamed cottage cheese or dry curd		
1/2 cup	grated parmesan cheese		

In large fry pan put 2 tbsp. oil - saute onion and garlic. Add meat - brown lightly - drain off excess fat.
Combine together - sugar - salt - oregano - rosemary and parsley.
Add to meat together with tomatoes and tomato sauce. Simmer 30 - 40 mins. - stir occasionally.
Cook noodles according to pkg. directions. Drain and rinse in cold water.
Place half of noodles in a 9x13" oven pan. Cover with 1/3 of sauce - half of mozzarella - half of cottage cheese. Repeat layers - and end with sauce on top. Sprinkle with parmesan cheese.
Bake @ 350° - 30 mins. Let stand 15 mins. before serving.
NOTE: If freezing DO NOT PUT PARMESAN ON TILL ready to bake.
VARIATION:
In place of sugar - salt - oregano - rosemary and parsley as called for in recipe - substitute using: 2 pkg. of spaghetti sauce mix.

Oma's Sauerkraut and Barley

1-28 oz. or 1 quart sauerkraut		1 lge.	onion - chopped
1 tsp.	pickling spices	3/4 cup	pearl barley
2 cups	water	2 tbsp.	brown sugar
2 lbs.	pork hocks - rib ends with meat or weiners		

Put all together in oven roasting pan - cover - bake @ 350° for one hour - stir occasionally. Uncover and bake 30 mins. more or till meat is tender.

NOTE: This was a special dish that Oma prepared whenever the family came together for special occasions.

Fried Rice

3 cups	cooked rice - hot	1 cup	cooked ham
5	eggs		bacon or shrimp
1/2 cup	green onions chopped	2-3 tbsp.	soy sauce
		1/2 tsp.	salt
1/4 tsp.	celery salt	1/2 tsp.	Accent (opt.)

Saute ham (bacon/shrimp) in a small amount of oil - remove from pan. Add onions - saute till soft - remove from pan.
Scramble eggs in more oil if needed.
Toss ingredients together in pan and serve.

Serves 6 - 8.

Rice Casserole

1 cup	raw rice	1 can	mushroom soup
1/4 cup	oil	3 cups	warm water
1 tbsp.	soya sauce	1 env.	onion soup mix
2 cup	cooked chicken or turkey - chunks		

Mix all ingredients together - put into a casserole dish.
Cover and bake @ 350° for 1 hour and 15 mins.

Elyce's Sunday Chicken

1 1/2 cup	Minute Rice
1/2 cup	milk
1 env.	dry onion soup mix
1-10 oz.	cream of celery soup
1-10 oz.	cream of mushroom soup
6-8	skinless - boneless chicken breasts

Grease large baking dish 9x13" - pour rice evenly into dish.

Heat celery and mushroom soup with milk until blended - pour over rice.
Lay chicken pieces over soup rice mixture and sprinkle with dry onion soup.

Seal with foil - bake at 325° for 2 hours plus.

VARIATION:
2/3 to 1 cup of regular rice may be steamed - then combined with soups to make the first layer in dish. Pieces of chicken may be browned before onion soup mixture is added. Bake as usual.

A regular frying chicken may be used in place of chicken breasts - lay pieces skin side up over the soup-rice mixture.

NOTE: The reason this recipe is called "Chicken on Sunday" is because you can put this dinner in the oven - go to church and when you arrive home it is ready for the family.

Chili Chicken

4-6	**chicken breasts - cooked and cubed**
1 pkg.	**taco chips**
1 lb.	**cheddar cheese - shredded**
1 sm.	**sour cream**
1 can	**cream of mushroom soup**
2 cans	**cream of chicken soup**
1 sm.	**diced Ortega chilis**

In a greased casserole dish - place in layers:

- chips   - cubed chicken   - sauce   - grated cheese

Repeat layers in order - bake @ 350° for 1 hour.

NOTE: A large can of diced chilis makes a spicier dish.

Turkey-Broccoli Casserole

3 cups	**cooked rice**
2 pkgs.	**broccoli spears - cooked slightly and drained**
1 can	**water chestnuts - drained**
1 can	**French fried onions**
3 cups	**diced turkey (more may be added)**

Mix together:
1-10 oz.	**mushroom soup**
1/2 cup	**mayonnaise**
1/2 cup	**milk**
1 - 2 cups	**diced cheese - Velvetta**

Sprinkle cooked rice on bottom of a flat greased casserole pan.
Place broccoli on top of rice and cover with turkey pieces.
Mix together soup - milk - cheese and mayonnaise. Pour the
soup mixture over the turkey mix - top with chestnuts.
Bake @ 350° for 30 - 40 mins.
Sprinkle on french onions and bake 5 mins. longer.
Remove from oven and let rest approx. 5 mins. before serving.

Itterman's Cabbage Rolls

4 cups	uncooked long grain rice (not instant)	1 1/2 tbsp.	salt
		1 1/2 tsp.	pepper
5 1/2 cup	water	4-5 med.	heads of cabbage
1 tsp.	salt	1 tbsp.	vinegar
1 1/2 lb.	ground pork	2 cans	tomato soup
1 1/2 lb.	ground beef	4-5 med.	onions - chopped

Cook rice in a covered saucepan with water over low heat.
Cook only till liquid is gone - DO NOT OVER COOK - set aside.

In a large bowl combine with hands - meat - spices and onions.
Add the cooled rice - mix well - mixture should stick together.

To prepare cabbage - remove cores - using a sharp knife.
Fill a large pot approx. half full of water - add vinegar - place in a
head of cabbage (one at a time). Cover and simmer about 5
mins. - or longer so that outer leaves can be removed with a fork -
continue to steam in this manner and remove leaves until they
become to small to use for rolls. Repeat this process for all
cabbage - drain well - cool - trim off excess core.

Place approx. 1 1/2 tbsp. of meat - rice mixture at the edge of
each leaf - start rolling up leaf tightly - folding in the sides as you
roll.
Place rolls - with seam side down into a greased 9x13" casserole
dishes. Single layer is best but double layers would be okay.
Cover and bake @ 350° for 35 - 40 mins.

Combine 2 cans of tomato soup with 1/4 cup of water - pour over
cabbage rolls. Cover and return to oven - bake 45 - 50 mins.
longer or till cabbage is fork tender and rolls begin to brown.
Makes approx. 125 rolls.

NOTE: If freezing some of these uncooked - lay them on a
slightly greased cookie sheet. Freeze until firm - place in ziplock
bags. When cooking frozen cabbage rolls allow an extra hour of
cooking time before adding tomato soup. These take a long time
to cook if frozen solid. If you have extra of meat mixture - make
"LAZY CABBAGE ROLLS". See recipe.

Egg Noodles

3	eggs	1 tsp.	salt
1/3 cup	water	2 1/4 cups	flour
3 tbsp.	oil		

Mix 3 eggs slightly together with water and oil. Measure flour and salt in a bowl - make a well in center. Add egg mixture - mix thoroughly with hands.

Turn dough onto a floured board - knead till smooth and elastic. Cover with plastic wrap and set in fridge to cool for 10 mins.

Dough should be firm yet able to roll out into 2 thin rectangles. These pieces should be placed on tea towels which maybe placed over back of chair etc.

Drying time approx. 1 hour. Dough must still be plyable enough to roll up as for a jelly roll.

With a sharp knife cut into thin slices - shake out cut slices on tea towels to dry - turn occasionally (must be completely dry before storing).

To cook - place into salted boiling water - boil till soft. Drain thoroughly - serve with butter - ketchup etc. or topping.

NOTE: The size of the eggs used in the recipe can make a difference of the flour quoted by 1/4 cup.

Topping: Delicious

1 cup fresh bread cubes - small pieces.
In pan - heat 1/2 cup butter till hot - add bread cubes.
Brown bread till crisp (careful not to burn).
Place noodles in a serving bowl - pour topping over.

This was a dish that was served with every meal when company came.

Pyrogy - Verinke

2 cups	warm water	6 tbsp.	sour cream
1/2 cup	cooking oil	6 cups	flour
2 tsp.	salt		

In a large bowl combine water - oil and salt. Beat with wire whisk. Gradually beat in flour and sour cream - using hands as it becomes stiff. After all the flour has been added - put on counter top - working mixture until you have a nice smooth dough and it has lost its stickiness. Put into a covered bowl and let rest while you prepare the fillings.

Roll out a portion of dough on a slightly floured surface - not too thin - like pie crust thickness. Using a round cookie cutter - cut into circles. Put approx. 1 tsp. of desired filling in center. Fold over to make a half circle and using floured hands - pinch together well.

Drop carefully into salted boiling water to cook. Don't over-crowd. Stir gently and let rise to top - boiling approx. 5 mins. Drain with a slotted spoon or colander. May be fried in butter if desired.

Serve with sour cream and bacon bits or sauerkraut fried in butter with onions.

Makes 50 - 60 pyrogies.

Table Grace:
For peaceful homes and happy days, for all the blessings God displays, we give thanks and praise.

Amen

Pyrogy - Verinke Fillings

Cottage Cheese:

2 lbs.	dry curd cottage cheese	1 tsp.	pepper
2 med.	onions - chopped fine	2	eggs
1 tbsp.	salt		

Combine the above ingredients and mix until it sticks together when squeezed. This makes approx. 100 pyrogy - depending on size.

Potato and Cheese:

1 med. onion - chopped finely	1 cup	grated cheddar cheese
2 cups cooked mashed potatoes		
1/2 cup sour cream	3/4 tsp.	salt
	1/4 tsp.	pepper

Combine above ingredients - mix so it sticks together - chill.

Dumpf Schupp Noodle
(Dumpling Casserole)

1 lb.	thick sliced bacon
	salt and pepper
1 1/2 cups	water
	bread dough - rolled in 1 1/2" balls
5 med.	potatoes - peeled - cut into large cubes
1 lge.	onion - sliced thin - separated

Line the bottom of a dutch oven or large pot with a single layer of bacon.
Spread potatoes even over bacon - sprinkle with salt and pepper - then onion rings - pour water over all this.

Top with bread dough balls - leave approx. 1 1/2" between each roll. Cover - cook on top of stove over low heat for approx. 1/2 - 3/4 hour. **DO NOT LIFT LID** until you hear the bacon frying for awhile. Serve with sour cream.

Oma's Kleizel

3 1/2 cups	mashed potatoes - smooth and no lumps
2	eggs
2 cups	flour
1 tsp.	salt

Into potatoes -stir in the eggs and flour.
Mix with hands to make a soft dough - place dough on a well floured surface.
Work dough turning often till it is soft but does not stick to hands - roll into 1" balls. Let rest on counter.

In a large pot bring water to a boil with 1 tsp. salt (as for pasta).
When water boils drop approx. 30 balls into the pot (2 at a time).
Cook approx. 5 mins. - remove from water with a slotted spoon - drain.

May be served with bread crumbs browned in butter.

Dumplings

Version #1

2	eggs - beaten
1 cup	milk
1 tsp.	salt
4 tbsp.	corn starch
2 cups	flour
2 tsp.	baking powder

Version #2

1	egg - beaten
2/3 cup	milk
1/4 tsp.	salt and pepper
2 tbsp.	melted butter
2 cups	flour

Combine eggs and milk - add in the remainder ingredients.
Drop by teaspoonfuls on hot stew - cover and bake approx. 20 mins.

NO PEEKING!

Itterman's Kleice

Large Spaetzle

2 tbsp.	lard/bacon drippings	2 1/2 tsp.	vinegar
	- room temperature	1 1/34 cup	warm water
1 1/2 tsp.	salt	1/4-1/2 cup	
butter/margarine			
6 cups	flour		

Combine in a bowl - lard - salt and flour - blend with a fork.
Gradually add combined water and vinegar - 1/2 cup at a time.
After water mix is added use hands and mix until dough forms a
large moist ball - place on a generously floured surface and
knead dough till flour is mixed in well - shape into a ball. Dough
will be soft - NOT STICKY - let rest 10 mins. Divide into 4
portions.

In a saucepan on stove bring to a boil approx. 3 qts. water.
Using a scissor cut dough into bite size pieces into the water.
Boil approx. 6-7 mins. or till Kleice come to the top - boil a few
mins. longer.

Pour into a colander - drain well - place into a serving bowl.

In a skillet melt and brown butter - you may crumble in cubes of
bread to brown.
Pour over Kleice - makes a nice topping when serving.

These resemble spaetzle except larger - use in place of pasta -
good with sauerkraut.
I like them with tomato juice poured over top - my family likes
ketchup.
These are definitely heavier than rice - maybe not so good before
participating in sports.

*The best time to accomplish something - is the
day before tomorrow.*

Notes:

The Salad Bar

Soups
Salads

Potato Soup

2	strips bacon - chopped	1 1/2 cup	diced potatoes
1 cup	chopped celery	1/2 tsp.	salt
1/2 cup	chopped onion	1 tsp.	chicken soup
3 cups	water		- dry mix

Fry chopped bacon - add celery and onion - saute till clear.
Add water - salt - potato and soup mix - cook till potatoes are soft.
Mash potatoes slightly - salt and pepper to taste.

VARIATION: Hash brown potatoes may be used.

Potato Dumpling Soup

(A depression soup.)

Potato Broth

3 cups	cubed potatoes
6 cups	water
1 tsp.	salt
1/4 tsp.	pepper
	cubed fried bacon

Drop Dumplings

1/3 cup	water(plus)
1/2 tsp.	salt
1 cup	flour
1/2 cup	milk
2 tsp.	vinegar

Combine potato broth ingredients except bacon. Cook till tender -
mash slightly.

For dumplings: combine water - salt and flour - mix until smooth.
(May have to add 2 - 3 tbsp. additional water.) With scant
teaspoonful of dough, dip into boiling potato broth. (Dough should
come off spoon easily.)

Simmer until dumplings are cooked - 10 - 15 mins.

Stir in milk and vinegar - simmer 5 mins. longer.

Add bacon.

Cabbage - Low Cal Soup

5 cups	water	1 tbsp.	margarine
1 tsp.	salt	4 cups	chopped cabbage
4 cups	diced potatoes	1 cup	chopped onion
1-28 oz. can	tomatoes	1 cup	chopped celery
1/2 cup	chopped fresh dill or		- optional
2 tbsp.	dry dillweed		salt and pepper

Combine potatoes - salt and water - cook until almost tender- do not drain.

In skillet melt margarine - saute cabbage - onion and celery- until limp and slightly browned.

Add tomatoes which have been slightly crushed.
Pour potatoes and water into the above vegetables.

Cook slowly for 1/2 hour - add dill - salt and pepper to taste.
Continue cooking for another 1/2 hour.

Makes 5 -6 servings.

VARIATION: Dry onion soup may be added for extra flavor.

Quick Macaroni - Tomato Soup

Cook macaroni according to package instructions and the number of servings (4).

When cooked - drain well.

In saucepan place 1 can tomato soup with 1 can milk.
Heat and add in the pre-cooked macaroni - salt and pepper to taste.

Cauliflower Cheese Soup

1 head	cauliflower (med. size)	1/4 cup	flour
1 tbsp.	chicken soup dry mix	2 cups	milk
2 cups	water	1 cup	grated cheese
1/4 cup	margarine	1/2 tsp.	dill weed (opt)
1/4 cup	chopped onion		buttered
1/2 tsp.	salt		bread cubes
1/8 tsp.	pepper		or croutons
			parsley

Cut cauliflower into small pieces. Add water and soup mix. Cook till tender. DO NOT DRAIN - set aside.

In saucepan melt margarine - add onion - saute till transparent.
Add salt - pepper and flour - stir in milk.
Heat until it boils and thickens - stirring occasionally.

Add cheese - stir to melt - combine mixture with cauliflower.

Garnish with croutons and parsley. Yields 5 cups.

VARIATION: Broccoli may be substituted for cauliflower.

Beef Barley Soup

(A thick soup.)

1/2 lb.	stewing beef (cubed) or	1 1/2 tsp.	salt
2 lbs.	soup bones with meat on	1 sm. can	tomatoes
6 cups	water	1/2 cup	pearl barley
1/2 cup	chopped onion	1	bay leaf
1 cup	chopped celery		
1 cup	diced carrots		
1	garlic clove - chopped		

Combine all ingredients in saucepan - bring to boil.
Simmer one hour or till barley is cooked - salt and pepper to taste.
If extra flavor is needed add beef soup dry mix.
Remove bay leaf before serving. Serves 4

Ham and Bean Soup

1 cup	dry navy beans	1 cup	potatoes - cubed
2 cups	water	1/4 tsp.	thyme
1/2 cup	chopped onion	1/2	bay leaf
1/2 cup	chopped celery		
6 cups	ham broth and meat		

Soak beans in water overnight - drain and rinse.

In saucepan combine - beans - broth - onion - celery - thyme and bay leaf.
Bring to boil - reduce heat - simmer one hour.

Add potatoes - simmer 30 mins. or longer till beans are cooked.

Salt and pepper to taste. Serve 4 - 6

Split Pea Soup

6 cups	ham broth	1 cup	split peas
1 cup	cubed ham	1 tsp.	chicken soup
1/2 cup	chopped onion		dry mix
1 cup	chopped celery	1/2	bay leaf
1 cup	shredded carrots	1 tsp.	tarragon
1 sm. can	tomatoes		

Combine all ingredients in saucepan.
Bring to a boil - simmer one hour.
Salt and pepper to taste.

NOTE: Homemade croutons flavored with Italian seasoning add flavor and texture when sprinkled on top of the soups.

Garden Vegetable Soup

1 cup	cut green beans	1 tsp.	dill weed
1 cup	diced carrots	3 tbsp.	ketchup
1 cup	peas	1/2 cup	cold water
1 cup	diced beets	2 tbsp.	flour
1/4 cup	chopped onions	1 tbsp.	margarine
3 cups	water	1 tsp.	vinegar
1 1/2 tsp.	salt	1/2 cup	chopped beet
			leaves when avail.
			salt and pepper

Place vegetables in saucepan - add water - salt and dill weed.
Cook till vegetables are tender - add ketchup.
Mix 1/2 cup cold water with flour till smooth - add to soup.
DO NOT BOIL.

Add margarine - vinegar - salt and pepper to taste.
Serve with a dollop of sour cream if desired.

VARIATION: Use fresh garden vegetables whenever possible.

French Onion Soup

1 lge.	thinly sliced onion	4 slices	toasted bread or
2 tbsp.	butter or margarine	2 cups	croutons
3 cups	beef broth	1/4 cup	parmesan cheese
1 tsp.	worcestershire sauce	1/4 cup	shredded swiss
1/4 tsp.	salt		cheese

In skillet - place butter - add onions - saute till clear and golden.
Add broth - sauce and salt - bring to a boil - simmer 15 mins.

Ladle into oven proof bowls - top with a slice of bread or croutons.
Sprinkle cheese over - place under broiler till cheese melts.

Serves 4

Exotic Chicken Salad

3 cups	mayonnaise	4 cups	seedless grapes (red/green) halved
3 tbsp.	lemon juice	1 can	water chestnuts (drained)
3 tbsp.	soya sauce		
8 cups	chicken/turkey (cooked and diced)	1 cup	slivered almonds (toasted - opt.)
7 cups	diced celery		salt and pepper to taste

Blend mayonnaise - lemon juice - soya sauce - salt and pepper.

Add chicken - celery - grapes and water chestnuts.
Toss lightly and chill minimum of 2 hours - overnight preferred.
Add slivered almonds just before serving. Serves 8 - 10.

NOTE: You may serve this on individual plates on a bed of leaf lettuce with a tomato wedge and several green or black olvies.

Ladies Luncheon
Exotic Chicken Salad served with:
    Melon and watermellon balls (in clear glass bowl)
    Hot roll and butter.   Dessert - Raspberry Sherbet

Taco Salad

1 lb.	ground beef	1	green pepper
1 pkg.	Taco Seasoning		- chopped
1 sm.	onion - chopped	1 head	lettuce - chopped
2-3	tomatoes - diced	1 cup	shredded cheddar
1 can	kidney beans		cheese
			taco chips - crushed
			Thousand Island or
			French salad dressing

In skillet brown meat - drain well. Add taco seasoning - let cool.

Add chopped onion - tomatoes - kidney beans and pepper.

In a large bowl - place lettuce - then add meat mixture.
Toss together.

Before serving add grated cheese and crushed Taco chips - toss.
Salad dressing may be added - opt..

Pistachio Dream Salad

1-14 oz. can	crushed pineapple
1-4 oz. pkg.	pistachio instant pudding
1 lge.	Cool Whip (4 cup)
3/4 pkg.	miniature marshmallows
1/2 cup	coconut (opt.)
1	banana
	seedless red grapes

Mix pineapple and juice with pudding - blend in Cool Whip.
Stir in the marshmallows and coconut - cover and refrigerate.

Before serving add red grapes and sliced banana.

Strawberry Cream Salad

1-6oz. pkg.	strawberry jello
2 cups	boiling water
1 1/2 cup	sour cream
1 cup	Cool Whip
2 cups	strawberries (fresh or frozen)

Dissolve jello in water - stir well.
Stir strawberries with juice into hot mix (if frozen berries are used).
Refrigerate till partially set.

Stir together sour cream and Cool Whip to blend.
Use a mixer on low speed to combine jello and sour cream mix.

If fresh berries are used - stir in - refrigerate to set completely.

Nut Pudding Salad

Grandma Decker

1 1/2 pkgs.	unflavored gelatine	3	egg yolks - beaten
1/4 cup	water		or 2 whole eggs
2 cups	milk	1/4 cup	sugar
1/4 cup	sugar	1 cup	whipping cream
		1/2 cup	chopped walnuts

Soak gelatine and water together - set aside.
In a saucepan bring milk and 1/4 sugar to a boil - very slowly add
the beaten eggs - stirring constantly - stir in gelatine mix.
Pour mixture into a salad bowl - let set partially.

Whip the cream using the 1/4 cup of sugar to sweeten.
Add the cream to the partially set mixture - fold in the nuts.

Refrigerate until set.

Layered 24 Hr. Lettuce Salad

1 head	lettuce - chopped	2 tsp.	sugar
1 med.	red onion - sliced thin	1 tsp.	salt
	separated	1/4 tsp.	garlic powder
1 cup	chopped celery	2 cups	Miracle Whip
10 strips	bacon - fried crisp - crumbled		
2 cups	frozen peas		

Measure out peas, place on paper towel to partially thaw and remove excess moisture - set aside.

In a large clear bowl place the following ingredients in layers - press down to compact - lettuce - onion - celery - bacon and peas.

Combine sugar - salt and garlic powder. Sprinkle over ingredients in bowl.

Spread Miracle Whip over salad - cover completely. Cover with plastic wrap and refrigerate for 24 hours.

Optional: Hard boiled egg slices may be added after the celery layer. Cherry tomatoes and shredded cheddar cheese may be used for garnish.

NOTE: This salad compacts as it marinates so extra Miracle Whip may need to be added before garnish and serving.

Whipped Cream Apple Salad

1 cup	whipping cream	8 tbsp.	powdered/icing sugar
1 tsp.	vanilla	5	apples
			(peeled - diced)

In a mixer bowl place cream - sugar - vanilla. Beat together until stiff. Stir in apples.

Yum Yum Salad

1-14 oz. can	crushed pineapple	1-3oz. pkg.	lemon jello
1 cup	water	1 cup	whipping cream - whipped
1/4 cup	sugar	1 cup	grated cheddar cheese

Combine in saucepan - pineapple with juice - water and sugar.
Heat until hot and sugar is dissolved - DO NOT BOIL.
Remove from heat - add jello and stir till dissolved.
Refrigerate until partially set.

Stir in whipped cream and cheese.
Refrigerate until firm.

NOTE: This is a favorite!

Plum Creek Fruit Salad

2	eggs - well beaten	1/2 cup	whipping cream
1/2 cup	sugar	2 cups	miniature marshmallows
2 tbsp.	flour	2	bananas - chunks
1-20 oz. can	pineapple chunks - drained - reserve juice	2	oranges - chunks
		1 cup	green grapes seedless

In a saucepan combine eggs - sugar - flour and pineapple juice.
Stir and boil until thickened - cool.

Whip cream till stiff - stir into cooled mixture.
Add marshmallows and fruits.

Oriental Cabbage Salad

1 head	cabbage - chopped	3 tbsp.	lemon juice
4	green onions - chopped	2 tbsp.	sugar
	(including tops)	1 tsp.	M.S.G. (opt.)
3/4 can	Smokehouse Almonds	3 tbsp.	seasoned
1 pkg.	instant noodles		rice vinegar
	- uncooked (chicken flavor)	1/2 tsp.	pepper
1 cup	cooking oil		

Combine in a container with a lid - oil - lemon juice - sugar - M.S.G. - vinegar and pepper. Shake well to mix.
Pour mix over cabbage and onions - refrigerate for several hours.
Just before serving - add almonds and noodles (broken).
This will add the "crunch" to the salad making it unique.

NOTE: You need to use smoked almonds - no substitute.
If seasoned rice vinegar not available - use white vinegar and add the seasoning package with noodles. (Optional - Add part or all of the seasoning package to the seasoned rice vinegar for extra flavor.)
VARIATION: 2 cups shredded cooked chicken maybe added to salad.

Cranberry Jewel Salad

1 lb.	cranberries	1/2 cup	walnuts -chopped
1 cup	sugar	1 cup	whipping cream
2 cups	mini marshmallows		- whipped or
2 cups	red seedless grapes	1 sm.	Cool Whip
	- halves		

In a food processor finely chop cranberries. Place in a bowl with the juice - add sugar - let stand 2 hours.

Add marshmallows - let stand 2 hours.

Add grapes (may use more than 2 cups if desired) and walnuts.
Fold in whipping cream. Refrigerate overnight.

Italian Garden Salad

1 head	Romaine lettuce		Croutons
1 med.	red onion	6-7	jalepeno peppers
1 can	black olives - drained		Italian salad dressing

Break lettuce into bite size pieces. Slice the red onion in circles - add the black olives and peppers. Toss salad - add enough Italian salad dressing for taste - top with croutons.
(Do not add the dressing until you are ready to serve the salad.)

Creamy Lettuce Salad

1/2 head	lettuce
1/2 cup	salad dressing
1/3 cup	light cream
3 tsp.	sugar
1 1/2 tsp.	vinegar

Wash and chop lettuce. In small bowl combine remainder of ingredients. Pour over lettuce and toss together.

Crunch Veggie Salad

2 cups	broccoli florets	1 1/2 tsp.	sugar
2 cups	cauliflower florets	1 tsp.	salt
2 cups	frozen green peas	1/4 tsp.	garlic powder
1 cup	chopped celery	1 cup	salad dressing
1 med.	red onion - thinly sliced	1 cup	shredded cheddar cheese
10-12	strips bacon - cooked crisp and crumbled		

Toss all vegetables together in a clear bowl. Mix together sugar - salt and garlic powder - sprinkle over vegetables - toss. Add the salad dressing - combine - cover and refrigerate overnight.
At serving time sprinkle with cheese and bacon. Serves 8 - 10.

Cucumber Salad

4-5 med.	**cucumbers or 6 cups sliced - packed**
1 med.	**onion - sliced thin and separated**
1/2 cup	**white vinegar**
1 tbsp.	**salt**
1/2 tsp.	**pepper**
1 tsp.	**sugar**

Place thinly sliced peeled cucumbers and onion into a large bowl. Set aside.

Mix together the rest of the ingredients - pour over vegetables.

Stir well - refrigerate several hours - drain off some liquid before serving.

NOTE: Serve as is or add 1/4 cup of sweet or sour cream.

Marinated Vegetable Salad

6	**tomatoes - cut in wedges**	**1 cup**	**diced celery**
3	**peppers - chopped (red-green-yellow)**	**2**	**carrots -sliced**
1	**red onion - sliced**		

Prepare vegetables - place in a large bowl.

Prepare Marinade:

2/3 cup	**vegetable oil**	**1/4 cup**	**vinegar**
1/4 cup	**green onion - cut fine**	**1 1/2 tsp.**	**salt**
1/2 tsp.	**pepper**	**1 tbsp.**	**sugar**
1/2 tsp.	**basil**	**1/2 tsp.**	**marjoram**
1/4 cup	**parsley chopped**		

Combine marinade ingredients - pour over vegetables.
Cover and refrigerate 4 hours or overnight - stirring occasionally.

NOTE: This dish goes well with many different meals - usually no left overs.

Brookdale Cole Slaw

1 med.	cabbage - shredded
1 tsp.	salt
2/3 cup	whipping cream - whipped
1/3-1/2 cup	vinegar
2/3 cup	sugar

Place shredded cabbage in covered dish in the refrigerator for several hours.

Mix ingredients in order given 30 minutes before serving. Pour over salad - chill and serve.

Frozen Strawberry Salad

1 lge.	Cool Whip
1 lge. pkg.	frozen strawberries
1-20 oz. can	crushed pineapple - drained
1 can	sweetened condensed milk
3	bananas - sliced

Mix all the above together and freeze in a 9x13" pan.

Take salad out of freezer approx. 1/2 hour before serving. Cut into squares and place in serving bowl.

Frozen Pineapple Nut Salad

2 env.	Dream Whip	1 cup	miniature
1-8oz. pkg.	cream cheese		marshmallows
1 cup	powdered/icing sugar	1 cup	chopped nuts
1-14oz. can	crushed pineapple		

Whip Dream Whip as per directions - set aside.

Whip cream cheese - add sugar - fold in undrained pineapple - marshmallows and nuts.
Blend together with Dream Whip - place in serving bowl.

Cover with plastic wrap and freeze overnight.
Take out of freezer several hours before serving.

VARIATION: Colored marshmallows may be used for special occasions.

Marinated Bean Salad

1-14 oz. can	kidney beans	1 tsp.	seasoned salt
1-14 oz. can	lima beans	1 tsp.	salt
1-14 oz. can	cut green beans	1/2 tsp.	pepper
1-14 oz. can	cut yellow beans	2/3 cup	vinegar
1 med.	onion -sliced thin	1/3 cup	oil

Rinse and drain kidney beans. Combine with other beans that have been drained. Add separated onion rings.

Mix together marinade made with the rest of ingredients.

Pour over the beans - toss together.

Place in refrigerator overnight - stir occasionally.

Pea Salad

2 pkg.	frozen peas (partially cooked)
1 cup	chopped celery
1 cup	grated sharp cheddar cheese
1/2 cup	chopped onion
1/2 cup	chopped peanuts
1/2 cup	sweet pickles - chopped
1/2 cup	mayonnaise
1/4 tsp.	salt

Do not overcook peas - drain. When cool add the rest of the ingredients that have been mixed together.

Cool well. If needed - add more mayonnaise before serving.

Creamy Fruit Salad

1 cup	pineapple juice	1-19 oz. can	pineapple chunks drained - reserve syrup
1/2 cup	sugar		
2 tbsp.	corn starch		
1	egg - beaten	oranges	- peeled and cubed
2 tsp.	lemon juice	apples	- peeled and cubed
1 lge.	Cool Whip	bananas	- sliced
		grapes	

In a saucepan stir together corn starch - sugar and pineapple juice. Add the beaten egg - cook til thickened.
Remove from heat - stir in lemon juice - chill.

Combine Cool Whip with chilled sauce. Toss together with fruits.

Holiday Salad

1-8 oz. pkg.	cream cheese
1-14 oz. can	crushed pineapple with juice
3 cups	miniature marshmallows
1 cup	whipping cream - whipped
1 cup	seedless grapes - halves
1 cup	pecans - chopped

Cream cheese together with a little of the pineapple juice till smooth.
Stir in the remainder of pineapple and marshmallows.
Fold in whipped cream - grapes and pecans - refrigerate overnight.

Strawberry Pretzel Salad

2 cups	pretzels - broken (1/2"-3/4" pieces)	1 cup	powder/icing sugar
		2 pkg.	frozen strawberries
3/4 cup	butter - melted		
1/4 cup	sugar	1-6oz. pkg.	strawberry jello
1-8oz. pkg.	cream cheese - softened	2 cups	boiling water
1-8oz.	Cool Whip		

Mix together pretzels - butter and sugar - press into a 9x13" pan.
Bake @ 350° for 6 mins. - Let cool.

Mix together - well beaten cream cheese and powdered sugar.
Stir in Cool Whip - spread over the pretzel crust.

Dissolve jello in boiling water - stir in strawberries and allow to cool. Pour strawberry mixture over cream cheese mix - refrigerate.

The pretzels "look" and "taste" like walnuts in this salad.

Twenty Four Hour 5 Cup Salad

1-14 oz. can	pineapple tidbits - drained
1-10 oz. can	mandarin oranges - drained
1 cup	coconut
1 cup	miniature marshmallows
1 cup	dairy sour cream
	chopped pecans - opt.

Combine and stir together pineapple - oranges - marshmallows - coconut and sour cream. Place into a serving bowl.

Sprinkle with chopped pecans - cover and refrigerate overnight.

Tomato Aspic

1-48 oz. can	tomato juice - divided	Miracle Whip Dressing
3 env.	unflavored gelatine	chopped walnuts

Mix together 2 cups tomato juice with gelatine - stir with fork to dissolve.

Pour remainder of tomato juice into a clear glass bowl and microwave on high 2 mins. - 15 sec. Stir dissolved gelatine mixture into hot mix - stir well.

Refrigerate till set - overnight if possible.

To serve - gently smooth Miracle Whip to cover - sprinkle with nuts.

Caesar Salad Dressing

1 cup	mayonnaise		1/2 tsp.	crushed garlic
	not Miracle Whip		2 tbsp.	parmesan cheese
3 tbsp.	milk		4	strips bacon
2 tbsp.	cider vinegar			- cooked crisp
	pinch of salt			and crumbled
				Croutons

Combine all ingredients except bacon and croutons - mix well.

<u>At serving time:</u>   Pour salad dressing over lettuce greens - toss lightly. Sprinkle on top of salad the prepared bacon bits and croutons. Unused portion of dressing may be put into a tightly closed jar and kept in refrigerator.

Potato Salad

2 lbs. med.	potatoes (approx. 5)	1 cup	salad dressing
2	green onions - sliced		(Miracle Whip)
	includes tops	1/4 cup	milk
3	hard boiled eggs	1 tbsp.	sugar
	- sliced	1 1/2 tbsp.	vinegar
1/2 cup	fresh dill	1 tsp.	salt
	- cut fine with scissors)		
1/4 tsp.	pepper		

Wash potatoes - boil in salted water with skins on till fork tender. Cool - take off skins - cut into cubes.

Place in a bowl - add onions - eggs and dill.
Mix together the rest of ingredients - pour over and toss to coat the potatoes.

Refrigerate for a few hours to blend flavors - preferably overnight.
Serves 4 or 5

VARIATION: Omit the green onions and dill - add 2 tbsp. green relish.

Macaroni Salad

4 cups	macaroni	1 tsp.	salt
1 cup	Miracle Whip	1/4 tsp.	pepper
1/4 cup	milk	3/4 cup	chopped celery
1 1/2 tbsp.	vinegar	3	green onions
1 1/2 tbsp.	sugar		- chopped

Prepare macaroni as to pkg. instructions - rinse in cold water - drain well. Mix together all ingredients - combine with macaroni. Refrigerate till serving time.

Ma's Cabbage Salad

1 med.	cabbage - shredded	2 tsp.	prepared mustard
1/2 cup	salad dressing	4 tbsp.	sugar
1/2 cup	light cream		pinch of salt
2 tbsp.	vinegar		

In small bowl combine salad dressing - cream - vinegar - mustard - salt and sugar - blend well. Toss cabbage and dressing together.
VARIATION: To the above you may add minced onion or chopped apple.

Broccoli Salad Delight

2-3	broccoli stalks	1/4 cup	raisins
1	green onion - chopped	1/2 cup	sliced almonds
1 cup	chopped celery	1 1/2 cups	salad dressing
2	slices bacon	1/4 cup	sugar
1/2 cup	sunflower seeds	4 tsp.	lemon juice

Cut broccoli fairly fine - place in a serving bowl with onion and celery. Fry bacon crisp and cumble. In a separate bowl combine - salad dressing - sugar and lemon juice - add all other ingredients - toss together.

Notes:

195

The Meat Market

Beef

Chicken

Fish

Pork

Old Fashioned Beef Stew

2 1/2 lbs.	round steak	1 tsp.	salt
1 tbsp.	oil	1/2 tsp.	pepper
2 tbsp.	butter or margarine	1 tsp.	thyme
3/4 cup	onion - finely chopped	1 tsp.	marjoram
1/4 cup	flour	1 cup	potatoes cubed
4 cups	beef bouillon made	1 cup	celery - chopped
	up of water and beef	1 cup	peas
	base granules	1 cup	carrots - sliced or chunks
		1/2 cup	chopped parsley - optional

Cut steak into 1" cubes - pat dry with paper towel. Heat oil and margarine in heavy skillet.

Brown meat well - one layer at a time (important) remove from pan - set aside.

Saute onions until golden in color - may need to add a little more margarine. Stir in the flour - brown - add in bouillon and seasonings.

Return meat to the pan - simmer partially covered till tender 1 - 1 1/2 hours.

This portion may be refrigerated overnight to allow flavors to blend or proceed by adding the vegetables (except peas) cook till tender 30 - 40 mins.. Add peas and parsley near the end of cooking time.

If the gravy is thin - mix together several tbsp. of flour and water in a jar. Slowly add and stir into stew mixture - cook till it bubbles and thickens.

If too thick - add water.

Add extra beef base granules if needed for flavor.

Gingered Beef Stir Fry

2 tbsp.	cooking oil	3 cups	broccoli - bite size
1/2 tsp.	garlic powder	3 cups	cauliflower - bite size
1 1/2 tsp.	ground ginger	1 tsp.	salt
4 tbsp.	oil	1/2 tsp.	pepper
1 med.	onion - wedges	2 tsp.	beef base granules
1 cup	celery		with 2 cups water
	- diagonally sliced	3 tbsp.	soya sauce
1 cup	carrots	2 1/2 tbsp.	corn starch
	- thinly sliced		
1 lb.	sirlion tip or inside round steak		

Thinly slice partially frozen meat across grain - refrigerate.
Prepare vegetables and set aside.

In a hot skillet place 2 tbsp. oil - add meat and seasonings.
Fry until brown stirring frequently - remove from pan.

Heat 4 tbsp. oil and fry vegetables - onion - carrots and celery.
These vegetables need longer cooking time - add brocolli -
cauliflower last. Beef broth may need to added to keep
vegetables cooking.
Vegetables should not be over cooked - still on the crisp side.

Add the corn starch to the rest of beef broth together with salt -
pepper and soya sauce. Stir into skillet to thicken and glaze the
vegetables.

Return meat to mixture in skillet - heat through.

This goes well served with white or brown rice - serves 3 - 4.
Chicken may be substituted for the beef if desired.

Chili

Great Taste

6 tbsp.	margarine or butter	3/4 tsp.	Tabasco sauce
5 med.	onions - sliced	3-14 oz.	cans tomatoes
3 lbs.	ground beef	1-9 1/2 oz.	tomato sauce
3 tbsp.	chili powder	1-5 1/2 oz.	tomato paste
1 tbsp.	salt	3-19 oz.	kidney beans
1 tsp.	paprika		

In a large skillet melt margarine - add onions - cook till tender.
Add ground beef - chili powder - salt - paprika and Tabasco
sauce.
When meat is cooked - add tomatoes - tomato sauce and tomato
paste.
Cover and simmer 45 mins. - add kidney beans - simmer 15 mins.
Serves 12.

NOTE: 5 cans of tomato sauce may be substituted for tomatoes -
tomato sauce and paste called for in recipe.
Canned tomatoes may be put into blender to take out chunks.

Meat Loaf

2	eggs - beaten	1/4 cup	onion - chopped
1 cup	milk	1 tsp.	salt
2/3 cup	bread crumbs	1/4 tsp.	pepper
2 lbs.	ground beef	1/2 tsp.	sage

Combine all ingredients - put into a loaf pan.
Make sauce - spread evenly over meat.

Sauce:

3 tbsp.	brown sugar	1/4 tsp.	nutmeg
1/2 cup	ketchup	1 tsp.	dry or prepared mustard

NOTE: Optional sauce: 1 can tomato soup diluted with 1/2 can of
water.

Bake @ 350° for 1 hour. Enjoy!

Barbecued Hamburgers

1 lb.	lean ground beef	1	egg
1 tsp.	salt	1 tsp.	onion powder
1/2 tsp.	pepper	1 tsp.	worcestershire sauce

Combine the above ingredients - shape into 5 patties.
Brush with BBQ sauce - cook on grill till done.

Serve with your favorite toppings - lettuce leaf - mustard - ketchup - relish - tomato slices - sauteed onions or Mayo Mix.

Saute onion in skillet: 2 tbsp. margarine and 2 cups chopped onions.

Mayo Mix: Combine - 1 cup mayonnaise - 1/4 cup chopped pimento - 10 oz. Velveeta cheese - cubed and 1 tbsp. sugar.

Oma's Kotletten (Hamburgers)

1 lb.	lean ground beef	1/4 tsp.	pepper
2	slices bread	1 tsp.	salt
1/4 cup	water	1/8 tsp.	nutmeg
1/4 cup	chopped onion	1	egg

Soak bread in water - squeeze out excess moisture.
Combine with remainder ingredients - shape into 8 patties.

In fry pan over medium heat - brown on both sides and cook till no longer pink inside.

VARIATION: Recipe as above: shape into 1 1/2" balls. Pour - 1 tin mushroom or tomato soup over top.

Bake @ 350° for 60 mins..

Oma's Beef Roast

5 lb.	chuck or blade beef roast
	salt and pepper
2	garlic cloves
1 lge.	onion - sliced

Rinse roast under hot tap water to seal in the juices.
Add salt and pepper to taste - brown meat in a hot oiled skillet -
both sides. Remove roast - place into a greased roasting pan -
add drippings. A little water may need to be added to the frying
pan to loosen drippings. Score the top of roast - insert the cloves
of garlic. Place sliced onions over top of roast.
Place roasting pan into a 425° oven for 25 mins. - lower oven to
300°. Bake for approx. 3 hours or till meat is tender - make gravy
using drippings.
NOTE: The grand children loved this roast - so delicious and
tasty.

Rouladen

6	thin slices sirlion steak		salt and pepper
6	slices bacon	3	dill pickles
1	onion - sliced		quartered lengthwise
2 cups	sour cream	1 tsp.	prepared mustard
2-3 Tbsp.	flour		consomme - opt.

Season meat slices with salt and pepper - both sides.
Spread mustard on each piece very thin. Place in the centre of
each piece bacon - onion - dill pickle - roll up and fasten with a
toothpick.
In a oiled hot skillet - brown meat on all sides - transfer to a
roasting pan. To drippings in pan add 1 cup water or consomme -
pour over the rolls.
Bake @ 325° until done - approx. 1 1/2 hours - remove meat.
Make a gravy by adding to the roasting pan 2 - 3 tbsp. of flour very
slowly - stirring - cook to thicken.
Remove from heat - stir in 2 cups sour cream.
NOTE: If gravy is too thick - add water for right consistency.

Sloppy Joe

1 lb.	ground beef	1 tbsp.	Worcestshire
1	chopped onion		sauce
1 can	chicken gumbo soup	1/4 cup	ketchup
1 tsp.	mustard		salt & pepper

In a skillet brown meat - drain well - add onion - cook together till onion tender.
Add remaining ingredients - simmer 15 - 20 mins. - serve on a hamburger bun.
NOTE: You may add some chopped celery if you wish.

Waikiki Meatballs

1 1/2 lbs.	ground beef	1 1/2 tsp.	salt
2/3 cup	fine bread crumbs	1/2 tsp.	ginger
	or cracker crumbs	1/4 cup	milk
1/3 cup	minced onion	1	egg

Combine all ingredients - mix well using hands - shape into 1" balls. Brown meat balls in a skillet and cook until done.

Sweet and Sour Sauce:

1-14 oz. can	pineapple tidbits	1/2 cup	white vinegar
	- reserve juice	2 tsp.	soya sauce
1 cup	brown sugar	1/3 cup	green pepper
	- packed		- opt.
2 1/2 tbsp.	corn starch		dash of pepper
1 cup	beef bouillon - 2 cubes		

In a saucepan prepare bouillon and bring to a boil.
Mix together sugar and corn starch - add to bouillon - stir in vinegar - soya sauce and reserved juice.
Add the meatballs to sauce - cook until thickened. Pour over meatballs. Stir in pineapple and peppers - heat only until meatballs are hot.

Swiss Steak

1 1/2 lbs.	round steak - trimed		salt and pepper
1/4 cup	ketchup	2 1/2 cups	water
1 lge.	onion - diced		flour

Cut steak into serving size pieces - salt and pepper - roll in flour.

With a little oil in a skillet - brown meat and add onions.

Transfer meat to a baking dish - pour over mixture of ketchup and water.

Cover and bake @ 350° - approx. 1 1/2 - 2 hours - a little more water may be needed for moisture.
Remove cover about 1/2 hour before you serve - to brown if needed.

VARIATION: Use same amount of steak - substitute ketchup mixture for 1 can of mushroom soup mixed with 1/2 can of milk. Pour over steak - bake as above. Amount of soup maybe doubled as it makes great gravy for potatoes.

Pepper Steak

1 1/2 lbs.	round steak	1/2 tsp.	garlic salt
4 tbsp.	oil	1/2 tsp.	pepper
2 lge.	tomatoes - chunks	1/2 tsp.	sugar
4	green peppers - chunks	2 tbsp.	corn starch
			dash of ginger
4 tbsp.	soya sauce		or more to taste
1 cup	beef bouillon/consomme		

Cut meat diagonally - against the grain - into thin slices - brown in hot oil. Stir in tomatoes - green peppers - soya sauce and seasonings. Cover and simmer till tender.
Blend together corn starch and consomme - stir into mixture - simmer for 10 mins. - serve over rice. Serves 6
NOTE: Canned tomatoes may be used.

Prime Rib Roast

6 lbs.   **roast - prime rib or standing rib roast**

Rub roast with combination of minced garlic and pepper.

Place meat in roasting pan - with fat side up - uncovered. Roast meat @ 325° allowing 30 mins. for each pound.

Season with salt one hour before roasting time is complete.

Remove from oven - let stand 15 - 20 mins. before carving.

Yorkshire Pudding

Prepare one hour before roast is done - set aside - let rest at room temperature.

1 cup	flour	1/2 tsp.	salt
1 cup	milk	2	eggs
	drippings		melted
			shortening

Combine ingredients - mix together with mixer till smooth.

When roast is removed from oven - increase oven to 450°.

Prepare a mixture of drippings and melted shortening to equal 1/2 cup - spoon into a 9x9" pan.

Place pan in oven and heat till hot - pour in batter - return to oven. Bake for 25 mins. or till puffy and golden.

Cut in squares - serve at once - makes 6 - 9 servings.

Strogonoff

1 lb.	beef (sirloin)	1 clove	garlic - minced
2 tbsp.	flour	2 tbsp.	margarine
3/4 tsp.	salt	2 tbsp.	flour
2 tbsp.	oil	2 tbsp.	ketchup
1 1/2 cups	fresh mushrooms - sliced	1 1/4 cup	water
1/2 cup	onion - chopped	1 tsp.	beef bouillon granules
1/2 cup	dairy sour cream		

Cut partially thawed meat - in bite size pieces.

Combine salt and 2 tbsp. flour - coat meat with flour mix.

Heat oil in skillet - add meat - brown quickly on both sides.

Add - mushrooms - onions and garlic.
Cook 3 - 4 mins. or until onion is crisp tender - remove meat and vegetables from pan. Add margarine to pan drippings - stir in 2 tbsp. flour - ketchup and beef granules.
Add water - cook until bubbly - stir and cook 1-2 mins. longer.

Return meat mix to pan - stir in sour cream.
Heat thro - BUT DO NOT BOIL - serve over hot noodles.
Serves 4.

Liver

Cut liver into serving pieces - salt and pepper - dredge with flour.

In a skillet add a little oil - heat until hot. Arrange liver in pan and brown both sides - over medium heat.
When liver is crisp on both sides it should almost be done.

Cut up an onion - smother liver with it.
Cook only till onions are tender.
NOTE: Nice topped with fried bacon strips.

Roast Turkey

1   **ready to cook turkey - approx. 14 lbs.**
        salt and pepper

Wash and dry turkey - rub cavity with salt and pepper.

Mix stuffing and fill cavity.

Put turkey with breast side up in roasting pan.
Wrap legs and wings with foil - pour 1 cup water into roaster.

Place in oven on lowest rack @ 350° for 1 hour.
Reduce heat to 325° for approx. 3 hours.
Baste often - if to brown cover loosely with foil.

Roasting time is approx. 25 mins. per pound.

Bread Stuffing

20 cups	bread cubes (day old)	3 tsp.	dry chicken soup
1 1/2 cups	margarine	3 tsp.	sage
2 cups	chopped celery	3 tsp.	poultry seasoning
2 cups	chopped onion	3 tsp.	salt
1 1/2 cups	water	1 tsp.	pepper

In skillet - saute celery and onions in margarine until transparent.

Mix spices with bread cubes - add sauteed mixture - toss
together.

Pour liquid over - mix together - stuff turkey.

NOTE: If to much dressing for cavity - wrap the rest in double
layers of foil - place along side of turkey in pan.

Dressing can also be cooked in a double foil lined pan.
Cover and bake @ 325° for 1 1/2 hours.

Chicken Cordon Bleu

2	chicken breasts	1/2 cup	flour
4 slices	swiss cheese	1 tsp.	salt
4 slices	ham - thin	1/2 tsp.	pepper
2 tbsp.	prepared mustard	1/4 tsp.	tarragon
1	egg - beaten	1/2 tsp.	paprika
1 tbsp.	water	1 cup	crushed corn
1/4 cup	melted butter		flakes or dry fine
			bread crumbs

Skin and debone breasts - cut in half.
Flatten chicken breasts between 2 pieces of waxed paper.
Spread mustard on each piece - layer with a slice of cheese and ham. Roll up in jelly roll fashion - secure with a toothpick.
Combine - flour - salt - pepper and tarragon - set aside.
Combine egg with water - roll each piece in flour mix - dip in egg.
Coat with a mixture of cornflakes - paprika and melted butter.

MICROWAVE - Arrange rolls in a circle on a plate - cover with wax paper. Microwave 2 mins. per roll on high or longer - let stand 5 mins. before serving.

Rolls may be browned in a fry pan and complete baking in oven until cooked.

Fried Chicken

	chicken pieces	1 tbsp.	dry mustard
	(washed - cut up)	1 tbsp.	thyme
2 tbsp.	salt	1 tsp.	ginger
2 tbsp.	pepper	1/2 tsp.	oregano
4 tbsp.	paprika	2	eggs - beaten
2 cups	flour		

Combine all dry ingredients in a dish. Dip chicken pieces in eggs - coat with flour mix.
In a pan brown chicken in hot oil. Put chicken into a roasting pan - bake @ 350° - 1 hour.

Baked Seasoned Chicken

1	frying chicken or desired pieces
	seasoned salt

Cut chicken into serving pieces - sprinkle generously with seasoned salt on all sides.
Place on greased baking sheet - skin side up.
Bake @ 350° - 1 hour and nicely browned.

Ginger Chicken

3 lbs.	chicken legs and thighs	1/2 tsp.	salt
1/3 cup	honey	1/4 tsp.	pepper
1/3 cup	chili sauce	1 tbsp.	corn starch
1/3 cup	soya sauce	2 tbsp.	water
1	tsp. ginger		

Microwave method:

Place chicken pieces in a baking dish.

Combine honey - chili sauce - soya sauce - ginger - salt and pepper.
Pour over chicken - cover and microwave 10 mins. on high heat.
Rotate dish - microwave 7 - 11 mins. longer.

Remove chicken from dish.

In bowl mix together corn starch and water - stir into sauce in the baking dish. Microwave uncovered till thickened. Pour over chicken to serve.

Oven method:

Prepare as above - bake @ 350° for 50 mins.
Baste frequently - remove chicken - prepare sauce as above.
Serves 4 - 6 people - serve with rice and green salad.

Elly's Glorious Chicken

1 can	mushroom soup	6 slices	ham - thin
1 cup	sour cream	6	chicken breasts
1 sm.	onion - chopped fine		- halves
		6 slices	bacon - halves (microwave to remove excess fat)

Line a slightly greased 9x13" glass oven proof dish with ham slices - then chicken breasts - top with bacon.

Bake uncovered for 30 mins. in a 350° oven.

Combine soup - sour cream and onion - spoon over meats. Return to the oven - bake uncovered for 1 hour.

NOTE: This recipe may be cooled and frozen after the 1st half hour of baking. Thaw slightly and continue to complete cooking process as above.

Salmon Loaf

2 cans	salmon - drained - reserve liquid	1/4 cup	chopped celery - opt.
2 cups	soft bread crumbs	1/2 tsp.	salt
1	egg - well beaten	1/4 tsp.	cayenne pepper
2 tbsp.	onion - minced	2 tbsp.	melted butter
2 tbsp.	parsley flakes	1/2 tsp.	baking powder
2 tbsp.	lemon juice		salad dressing

In bowl place salmon - flake with a fork.
Combine reserve liquid plus salad dressing to equal 1/2 cup. Add this and all other ingredients to salmon.
Shape into a loaf - place into a lightly oiled foil lined baking dish.

Bake @ 375° - 40 mins. - unmold on serving platter - garnish with lemon slices - sprinkle with parsley - surround with green peas.

Baked Salmon

1 lge.	whole salmon - cleaned and towel dried lemon juice salt and pepper	1	onion - thickly sliced butter parsley flakes

Prepare a baking dish with thick layers of foil - well buttered.

Season fish with salt and pepper inside and out.

Place inside of cavity - butter - parsley and onion.
Squeeze lemon juice over fish.

Wrap fish well in the buttered foil. Close and fold so no steam can escape during baking.

Bake @ 400° for approx. 30 - 35 mins.

Fish is cooked when flesh easily flakes with a fork.

Delicious served with tartar sauce - scalloped potatoes and salad.

NOTE: This fish can be barbecued with extra layers of foil. BBQ approx. 15 mins. per side.

Stuffing for Fish:

2 tbsp.	minced onion	1 tbsp.	dried parsley
1/4 cup	chopped celery		flakes
2 1/2 tbsp.	melted butter	1 tsp.	salt
2 cups	day old bread crumbs	1/8 tsp.	thyme
		1 tbsp.	hot water

Combine ingredients - stuff fish cavity. Bake as above.

To serve: Garnish with lemon slices and parsley.
Serve with tartar sauce (page 148) with the added tomato.

Deep Fried Fish

2-3 lbs.	fish fillet - firm white fish
	milk
2 tbsp.	lemon juice or 1 lemon sliced
2 cups	flour
1 tsp.	sweet basil
1 tsp.	pepper
1/2 tsp.	garlic salt

Cut fish fillets into serving size pieces - place in a shallow pan - cover with milk and lemon.

Let marinate for 1/2 hour or more - drain.
Roll fish in flour - dip into batter (below) - deep fry till golden brown.

Fish Batter:

2 1/2 - 3 cups	pancake flour mix
4 cups	club soda

Deep fry in 3 cups vegetable oil.

VARIATION: **Pan Fried Fish**
Salt and pepper fish fillets - dip in flour - pan fry in hot fat.

Pork Roast

2 1/2 - 3 lbs.	loin or shoulder of pork	2 tsp.	salt
1/4 tsp.	sage - opt.	1/2 tsp.	pepper
1/4 tsp.	rosemary - opt.	1 clove	garlic
1/4 tsp.	thyme - opt.		

Rub roast well with combined seasonings.
Place fat side up in roasting pan - add garlic cloves.
Bake @ 350° for 30 mins. - reduce heat to 325°.
Allow 25 mins. for each pound.
Serve with applesauce.

Baked Ham

1	ready to eat ham	2 cups	water

Score fat surface of ham - place in roasting pan fat side up - add water.
Bake @ 325° - 20 mins. per pound.
During last half hour of baking - baste every 10 mins. with glaze.

Ham Glaze:

1 cup	brown sugar	2 tsp.	dry mustard
3 tbsp.	flour	3 tbsp.	vinegar

Mix together - if too thick - add fruit juice.
Serve with pineapple slices.

Pork Chops with Gravy

6	pork chops - 3/4-1" thick	1/2 tsp.	ginger (opt.)
2 tbsp.	cooking oil	1/4 tsp.	rosemary
1 can	mushroom soup	2/3 cup	chicken broth
3/4 tbsp.	flour	1 can	french fried
1 tsp.	salt		onions (divided)
1/2 tsp.	pepper	1/2 cup	sour cream

In skillet heat oil - brown chops (4 - 5 mins. per side).
In a 9x13" baking dish place chops in a single layer.
Mix together mushroom soup - flour - salt - pepper - ginger - rosemary and chicken broth - pour mixture over the chops.
Sprinkle with half of onions.

Cover and bake @ 350° - 45 mins.

Remove from oven to stir in 1/2 cup sour cream.
Sprinkle with remainder onions. Return to oven uncovered - bake for 10 mins. - Serves 6

Sweet and Sour Spareribs

2-3 lbs.	spareribs	3 tbsp.	vinegar
2 tbsp.	flour	1 cup	ketchup
1/2 tsp.	dry mustard	1 cup	water
1/4 cup	sugar	1	garlic clove
2 tbsp.	soya sauce		crushed
	salt and pepper	3 sm.	onions - chopped

Bake ribs for 1/2 hour in a 325° oven - to remove excess fat.
Drain well - cool - cut into small pieces.
Place drained ribs into roasting pan - combine all ingredients for
sauce - add to the ribs.
Cook slowly in a 325° oven for one hour or till done.

Serve with rice and a tossed salad.

Glazed Rack of Ribs

3-4 lbs.	spareribs	1/2 cup	marmalade
1 tsp.	salt	1 tbsp.	water
1 clove	garlic		BBQ sauce

Place rack of ribs - salt and garlic in cooking pot.
Cover with water - cook 45 mins. Drain and let dry.

Mix marmalade with water - brush on meaty side.
Spread your favorite BBQ sauce on both sides - be generous.

BBQ on grill or 6 inches below broiler until browned. Serves 4

Barbecued Pork

Restaurant Style

2	whole pork tenderloins (about 12 oz. each)	1 tbsp.	honey
1/4 cup	soya sauce	1 tsp.	red food coloring
2 tbsp.	dry red wine	1/2 tsp.	ground cinnamon
1 tbsp.	brown sugar	1 clove	garlic - crushed

Remove and discard fat from meat.

Combine soya sauce - wine - sugar - honey - food coloring - cinnamon and garlic in a large bowl.

Add pork - turning tenderloins to coat complete.
Cover and let stand at room temperature for 1 hour - turning occasionally.
Drain pork - reserve marinade - bake in preheated 350° oven - approx. 45 mins.

Turn and baste frequently with reserve marinade.
Remove from oven - cool - cut into diagonal slices.

Porkies

1 lb.	ground ham	**Basting Sauce**	
1 1/2 lbs.	ground pork	1 1/2 cups	brown sugar
2	eggs - beaten	1/2 cup	water
1 cup	milk	1/2 cup	vinegar
1 cup	quick oatmeal	1 tbsp.	dry or prepared mustard
	salt and pepper		

To the ground meats add eggs - salt - pepper - oats and milk.
Shape into 10 oblong "Porkies".
Bake @ 350° for 1 hour.
Baste with basting sauce during baking time.
To Serve: Top with a pineapple tidbit and a maraschino cherry.

Garlic Honey Ribs

Country Style

4 lbs.	country style ribs	1/2 cup	honey
3	garlic cloves minced	1/4 cup	soya sauce
1/2 cup	ketchup	1/4 cup	cold water
		2 tbsp.	corn starch

Place ribs in a roasting pan - cover.
Bake in oven @ 350° till partially - almost cooked - drain.

In a saucepan combine corn starch and water - make smooth
paste - add ketchup - honey -soya sauce and garlic.
Simmer together till slightly thickened.

Pour over ribs during last 1/2 hour of baking.

Husband's Menus

Home Alone Cooking

Roy - (Sylvia)　　　**Eyebrow, SK**　　　**Canada**

Bowl of Bread Cubes with Sugar and Milk - Bologna - Scrambled Eggs. All of the above covered with strawberry jam - as long as it sticks.

Don - (Alice)　　　**Tacoma, WA**　　　**U.S.A.**

Peanut Butter - Sour Dough Bread Toast - Bacon - Green Beans - Terriyki Chicken.

Gordon - (Ann)　　　**Ardrossan, AB**　　　**Canada**

Grated Carrots with Sugar and Cream - Scrambled Eggs - Bread and Jam - Fried Steak and Fish.

Elmer - (Elma)　　　**Sherwood Park, AB Canada**

Boiled Eggs - Pork and Beans - Bologna and Salmon. A large bowl of ice cream covered with chocolate sauce.

Inquiries:

Crossroads Country Recipes
Box 117
Eyebrow, SK
Canada S0H 1L0

ALL THINGS BEING EQUAL

EQUIVALENTS

1 cup	= 1/2 pint	3 tsps.	= 1 tbsp.
2 cups	= 1 pint	4 tbsps.	= 1/4 c.
4 cups	= 1 quart	5-1/3 tbsps.	= 1/3 c.
4 quarts	= 1 gallon	8 tbsps.	= 1/2 c.
8 quarts	= 1 peck	16 tbsps.	= 1c. or 8 oz.
4 pecks	= 1 bushel	1 cup	= 8 fl. oz.

EMERGENCY SUBSTITUTIONS

1 square chocolate	=	3 tbsps. cocoa & 1 tbsp. butter
1 tbsp. corn starch (for thickening)	=	2 tbsps. flour
1 c. buttermilk	=	1 c. yogurt
1 c. milk	=	1/2 c. evaporated milk & 1/2 c. water
1 c. sour milk	=	1 c. milk & 1 tbsp. lem. juice or vinegar
1 c. of cake or pastry flour	=	1 c. all-purpose minus 2 tbsps.
1 tsp. baking powder	=	1/4 tsp. bkg. soda & 1/2 tsp. cr. of tartar
1 c. sugar	=	1 c. honey-use 1/4 c. less liquid in recipe
1 c. brown sugar	=	1 c. granulated sugar
1 c. oil	=	1/2 lb. butter or margarine
1 tbsp. prepared mustard	=	1 tsp. dry mustard
1 clove garlic	=	1/8 tsp. garlic powder

PASTA & RICE
Macaroni:
1 c. uncooked = 2 1/2 c. cooked

Noodles: 1c. uncooked = 1 c. cooked

Spaghetti: 8 oz. uncooked = 4 c. cooked

Rice: 1 c. uncooked = 3 c. cooked

HERBS
1 tsp. dried = 1 tbsp. fresh

DAIRY
Cheese:
4 oz. = 1 c. shredded
1 lb. = 4 c. shredded
Butter:
1 stick = 1/2 c.
4 sticks = 2 c. = 1 pound

MEASURES

English	Metric
1/4 teaspoon	1 ml
1/2 teaspoon	2 ml
1 teaspoon	5 ml
1 tablespoon	15 ml
2 tablespoons	25 ml
1/4 cup	50 ml
1/3 cup	75 ml
1/2 cup	125 ml
2/3 cup	150 ml
3/4 cup	175 ml
1 cup	250 ml
1 1/2 cups	375 ml
2 cups	500 ml

SUGAR

1 lb. granulated sugar	=	2 c. granulated sugar
1 lb. brown sugar	=	2 1/4 c. brown sugar - packed
1 lb. confectioners' sugar	=	3 1/4 c. confectioners' sugar

CRUMBS

1 slice of bread	=	1/2 c. crumbs
14 graham cracker squares	=	1 c. crumbs
18 chocolate wafers	=	1 c. crumbs
22 vanilla wafers	=	1 c. crumbs

POPCORN

1/4 c. unpopped	=	5 c. popped

WEIGHTS

For Fish, Meat, Poultry and Bulk Fruits and Vegetables

English	Metric
1 ounce	28 g
1/4 pound or 4 ounces	125 g
1/2 pound or 8 ounces	250 g
3/4 pound or 12 ounces	375 g
1 pound	500 g
2.2 pounds	1 kg

Fold:
To add ingredients by lifting gently from underneath and folding over with a rubber spatula.

Baste:
To moisten foods while they are cooking.

Dollop:
A heaping spoonful of garnish used as topping - (sour cream or whipped cream).

Blanch:
To place into boiling water - steam 2 - 3 mins.

Saute:
To cook in a small amount of fat in a skillet.

Par-Boil:
To boil in liquid until partially cooked.

Garnish:
To decorate - usually an edible food - (accompaniment).

Drizzle:
To pour a thin stream of liquid slowly over food.

Index

All Things Being Equal
Substitutions 217

Appetizers
Cheese Ball 19
Cheese Dip 19
Dry Ribs 24
Elyce's Hot Chicken
Wings 20
Fruit Dip 21
Hot Artichoke Dip 20
Salmon Pate 21
Sausage Rolls 23
Seafood Dip 22
Shrimp Cracker Dip 23
Spinach Dip in Bread
Basket 22
Veggie Dip 20

Bars - Squares
Almond Bars 84
Brownies 80
Cherry Bars 81
Cherry Slices 80
Chip Caramel Bars 86
Choco Cherry Bars 85
Date Bars 83
Fudgy Brownies 81
Lemon Squares 78
Marzipan Bars 84
Peanut Butter Bars 78
Rice Krispie Caramel
Bars 79
Rocky Road Bars 85
Turtle Bars 82

Basics - How To
General Tips 13

Beverages
Apple Cider 27
Cherry - Orange
Kool-Aid Punch 29
Clear Punch 28
Cranberry Sherbet
Punch 25
Grape Fizz 28
Hot Chocolate -
Cocoa Mix - Dry 25
Hot Chocolate 25
Milk Shakes 27
Orange Julius 27
Raspberry - Cranberry
Punch 26
Smith Iced Tea 26
Solar (Sun) Tea 28
Sunshine Wedding
Punch 30
Tropical Punch 29
Wassail (Non-Alcoholic) . 28

Biscuits
Baking Powder Biscuits . 96
Corn Bread 96

Breads - Yeast
Bake Day Surprises . . . 109
Basic Bread or Buns . . . 102
Cinnamon Buns 106
Doughnuts 111
Elephant Ears 109
Elly's Yeast Buns 105
Enae's Twisters - Umges 112
French Bread 104

Fruit Kuchen and Gusse 110
Hot Cross Buns 113
Itterman's Paska 115
Monkey Bread 107
Poppy Seed Bread 114
Scuffles 113
Sweet Dough Variations 108
Sweet Roll Dough 107
Whole Wheat Bread ... 103

Brunch

Chicken a la King 44
Crepes 43
Eggs Benedict with
Hollandaise Sauce 41
Elyce's Coffee Cake 46
French Toast 39
Ham and Cheese
Brunch 39
Oma's Phlinzen
- Pancakes 40
Oma's Potato Pancakes . 40
Omelets 45
Pancakes 43
Waffles 42

Cakes

Apricot Crumble Cake .. 64
Black Forest Cake 63
Carrot Cake 60
Gumdrop Fruit Cake 68
Laisy Daisy Oatmeal Cake57
Light Fruitcake 67
Lovelight Chiffon Cake .. 58
Oma's Crumb Cake 65
One Bowl Chocolate Cake64
Popcorn Cake 61
Poppy Seed Cake 62
Puffed Wheat Cake 61
Raisin Cake 60
Rhubarb Cake 57
Spiced Coffee Cake 66
Springtime Sponge Cake 59

Candy

Chocolate Almond Brittle 32
Chocolate Covered
Pretzels 33
Delicious Microwave
Fudge 35
Dipped Chocolate
Coconut Balls 31
English Almond Toffee .. 34
Nuts and Bolts 31
Oven Caramel Corn 33
Poppycock or Popcorn
Balls 36
Turtles 32

Casseroles

Canton Noodle Dish ... 163
Chili Chicken 166
Dumpf Schupp Noodle . 170
Dumplings 171
Egg Noodles 168
Elyce's Sunday Chicken 165
Fried Rice 164
Itterman's Cabbage
Rolls 167
Itterman's Kleice 172
Kidney Bean Casserole 162
Lasagna 163
Lasy Cabbage Rolls ... 162
Mexican Casserole 161
Oma's Kleizel 171
Oma's Sauerkraut and
Barley 164
Pyrogy - Verinke 169
Pyrogy - Verinke Fillings 170
Rice Casserole 165
Turkey - Broccoli
Casserole 166

Cookies

Chipnut Choodles 75
Date Balls 74

Ebea's Chocolate Chip
Cookies 69
Gingersnaps 73
Gumdrop Cookies 76
Jam - Jam Cookies 71
Maple Puffs 75
Marshmallow Caramel
Balls 70
Meringues 77
Molasses Cookies 73
Neopolatin Cookies 70
Oatmeal Date Filled
Cookies 72
Oatmeal - Raisin Cookies 69
Peanut Butter Blossoms . 74
Shortbread 76
Sugar Cookies 71

Desserts
Apple Coffee Cake
Dessert 132
Banana Split Dessert . . 124
Caramel - Apple Raisin
Dessert 121
Cheesecake 120
Cherry Cheesecake
Supreme 124
Chocolate Cream Roll . 129
Chocolate Mousse
Dessert 130
Cool Fruit Pizza
or Tarts 133
Decadent Apricot
Cheesecake 119
French Vanilla Torte . . . 126
Fruit Cocktail Dessert . . 134
German Torte 122
Layered Mousse
Dessert 131
Lemon Jello Dessert . . . 123
Peanut Buster Parfait . . 128
Rhubarb Meringue
Dessert 125
Strawberry Shortcake . . 123

Supreme Cherry
Bombe 126
Triffle 127

Frostings - Fillings
Caramel Icing 141
Chocolate Icing 143
Chocolate Satin
Frosting 144
Coffee Cream Filling . . . 144
Coffee Whip Icing 142
Cream Cheese Icing . . . 142
Lemon Cream Filling . . 143
Mocha Icing 143
Pudding Icing 141
Royal Icing 141
White - Chocolate
- Mocha Icing 143

Husband's Menus 216

Loaves
Banana Loaf 99
Coconut Cherry Loaf . . . 99
Date Loaf 101
Graham Nut Bread 100
Lemon Loaf 101
Pumpkin Bread 100

Meats
Beef
Barbecued Hamburgers 200
Chili 199
Gingered Beef Stir Fry . 198
Liver 205
Meatloaf 199
Old Fashioned Beef
Stew 197
Oma's Beef Roast 201
Oma's Kotletten 200
Pepper Steak 203
Prime Rib Roast 204
Rouladen 201

Sloppy Joe 202
Strogonoff 205
Swiss Steak 203
Waikiki Meatballs 202
Yorkshire Pudding 204
Chicken
Baked Seasoned
Chicken 208
Bread Stuffing 206
Chicken Cordon Bleu . . 207
Elly's Glorious Chicken . 209
Fried Chicken 207
Ginger Chicken 208
Roast Turkey 206
Fish
Baked Salmon 210
Deep Fried Fish 211
Salmon Loaf 209
Pork
Baked Ham 212
Barbecued Pork 214
Garlic Honey Ribs 215
Glazed Rack of Ribs . . . 213
Pork Chops with Gravy . 212
Pork Roast 211
Porkies 214
Sweet and Sour
Spareribs 213

Menus 9

Muffins
Bran Muffins 97
Oatmeal Muffins 97
Sunrise Muffins 98

Pies - Tarts
Apple Pie 93
Baked Pastry Shell 88
Blueberry Pie 92
Butter Tarts 88
Cherry Pie . . . . : 91
Coconut Jam Tarts 95
Elyce's Cream Pie Filling 89
Flapper Pie 90

Glazed Strawberry Pie . . 91
Lemon Pie 93
Never Fail Pie Pastry . . . 87
Pecan Pie 94
Pumpkin Pie 92
Raisin Pie 94
Refrigerator Pie Pastry . . 87
Sour Cream Raisin Pie . . 95

Puddings
Bread Pudding 136
Chocolate Fudge
Pudding 137
Christmas Pudding 135
Creamy Rice Pudding . 136
Saucy Raisin Pudding . 137

Salads
Broccoli Salad Delight . 194
Brookdale Cole Slaw . . 188
Caesar Salad - Dressing 193
Cranberry Jewel Salad . 185
Creamy Fruit Salad 190
Creamy Lettuce Salad . 186
Crunch Veggie Salad . . 186
Cucumber Salad 187
Exotic Chicken Salad . . 180
Frozen Pineapple
Nut Salad 189
Frozen Strawberry Salad 188
Holiday Salad 191
Italian Garden Salad . . . 186
Layered 24 Hour
Lettuce Salad 183
Macaroni Salad 194
Marinated Bean Salad . 189
Marinated Vegetable
Salad 187
Ma's Cabbage Salad . . 194
Nut Pudding Salad 182
Oriental Cabbage Salad 185
Pea Salad 190
Pistachio Dream Salad . 181
Plum Creek Fruit Salad 184

Potato Salad 193
Strawberry Cream Salad 182
Strawberry Pretzel Salad 191
Taco Salad 181
Tomato Aspic 192
Twenty Four Hour
5 Cup Salad 192
Whipped Cream
Apple Salad 183
Yum Yum Salad 184

Sandwiches
Bacon Cheese
Broiler Buns 49
Bacon Egg on a Muffin . . 48
Sandwich Fillings 47

Sauces
Sweet - Savory - Gravies - Marinades
Applesauce 146
Barbecue Sauce 150
Beef Marinade 147
Caramel Sauce 145
Chicken Marinade 148
Chocolate Sauce 145
Croutons 146
Easy Caramel Sauce . . 145
Honey Mustard Sauce . 150
Marinade for Salmon . . 148
Plum Sauce 150
Pork Marinade 147
Quick Gravies 149
Tartar Sauce 148
White Sauce 149

Snacks
Bruchetta 51
Focaccia Bread 51
Garlic Bread 49
Gourmet French Bread
Topping 54
Grilled Patti Melt on Rye   50

Nachos 49
Parmesan Cheese Bread 53
Quesadillas 53
Quiche 52
Tuna Melt 52
Tuna Ring 50

Soups
Beef Barley Soup 177
Cabbage - Low
Cal Soup 176
Cauliflower
Cheese Soup 177
French Onion Soup . . . 179
Garden Vegetable Soup 179
Ham and Bean Soup . . 178
Potato Dumpling Soup . 175
Potato Soup 175
Quick Macaroni - Tomato
Soup 176
Split Pea Soup 178

Vegetables
Baked Onions 157
Broccoli Bake 155
Brown Baked Beans . . . 157
Corn on the Cob 155
Glazed Carrots 158
Green Bean Mandarin . 158
Harvard Beets 153
Hash Brown Bake 159
Scalloped Corn 156
Scalloped Potatoes . . . 154
Scalloped Potatoes . . . 153
Sliced Potato Bake 159
Stuffed Baked Potatoes 160
Sweet and Sour
Cabbage 156
Whipped Potato Dish . . 161
Yummy Yams 157